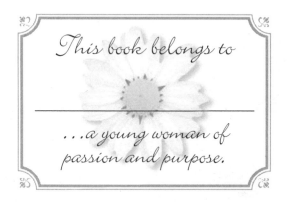

This book belongs to

_____

...*a young woman of
passion and purpose.*

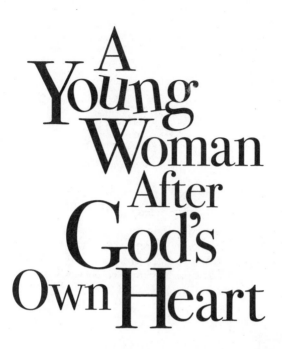

A Young Woman After God's Own Heart

Elizabeth George

HARVEST HOUSE™ PUBLISHERS

EUGENE, OREGON

Cover by Garborg Design Works, Minneapolis, Minnesota

Acknowledgments

As always, thank you to my dear husband, Jim George, M.Div., Th.M., for your able assistance, guidance, suggestions, and loving encouragement on this project.

A YOUNG WOMAN AFTER GOD'S OWN HEART

Library of Congress Cataloging-in-Publication Data
George, Elizabeth, 1944–
    A young woman after God's own heart / Elizabeth George.
        p. cm.
Summary: Inspirational chapters and bible study citations present a pathway to a closer relationship with God.
    ISBN 0-7369-0789-0 (pbk.)
    1. Teenage girls—Religious life—Juvenile literature. 2. Girls—Religious life—Juvenile literature. 3. Christian life—Juvenile literature. [1. Prayer books and devotions. 2. Christian life.] I. Title.
    BV4551.3 .G46 2003
    248.8'33—dc21
                                                                                2002013479

Contents

Your Education

Your Service to Others

Your Self

Part Three

The Practice of God's Priorities

This book is lovingly dedicated to
the "young women" in my life,
my cherished granddaughters,

∽

Taylor Jane Zaengle
Katherine Elizabeth Seitz

∽

May you walk in
all God's ways.

~ *Proverbs 3:6* ~

A Word of Welcome

Dear Friend,

Without even meeting you, I can tell you are someone very special! Why? Because you're choosing to read this book. When you consider its title, it becomes pretty obvious that you desire to become a woman after God's own heart. This book is packed with information and how-to's that will show you how to fulfill the desires of your heart—how to become a woman after God's own heart. As we begin our journey together, a few things will make it even sweeter.

Open your book... and enjoy it! Everything you need is here. I've tried to make it convenient for you as a busy young woman. In my mind I've pictured you reading this book on your bed at home, in a bunk bed at camp, in the backseat of the car or on an airplane while on your family vacation, in a lounge chair sunbathing around a pool, even in the library after you've finished your homework. Enjoy your book, carry it with you, and let God's Word instruct you.

Open your heart... to your friends. Encourage them to get books too. Then you will each be growing, which means your friendships will be growing in the right direction—in the things of the Lord. A godly woman needs other godly women as friends. So invite them to join you.

Open your heart... and look around. Are there any girls you don't know very well at school, or in the neighborhood, or perhaps where you work, that you can invite to join you in your study? Girls who need the Savior? Who need some guidelines for their lives? Who need a friend? Whisper a prayer to God, be bold, and reach out and invite someone you'd like to know better to get together.

Open your heart... to the priorities and topics covered in this book. They are tailor-made just for you. They'll give you God's wisdom and guidelines for the major areas of your life.

Open your heart... through prayer to the Holy Spirit. Ask Him to illuminate His Word, to help you understand God's plan and priorities for your life, and to transform your heart.

Open your heart... and dream! Dream of the woman you yearn to be—a woman after God's own heart.

And now let's put feet on those dreams! It is the prayer of my heart that the contents of this special book will encourage you, excite you, instruct you, and inspire you to follow after God's own heart even more passionately.

In His great and amazing love,
Your friend and sister in Christ,

Elizabeth George

Part One

The Pursuit of God

1

A Heart
Devoted to God

*But only one thing is needed. Mary
has chosen what is better, and it will
not be taken away from her.*

LUKE 10:42

Have you ever felt nervous...fidgety...on edge...
cranky? Sort of like your life was falling apart and
you were losing control? And even though you
knew it and you didn't want to act the way you were, you
kept on stomping through your day, lashing out at anybody
and everybody who crossed your path—your parents,
your brother or sister, your friends, a salesperson?

Well, my new friend, you are not alone! This happened
to a woman in the Bible—a woman just like you and me—
who got too worked up. In fact, she was a wreck! Her
name is Martha, and Martha was a friend of Jesus.

What Happened?

What happened to put Martha over the edge? In a few
words, Jesus and His disciples were coming to her house.

11

Wow! Now *that* should have been the best day of Martha's life! But Martha went into a tailspin. Why? Because Martha got too involved in the activities of her life—activities like…

> *serving* Jesus and
>
> *working* for Jesus.

And in all her serving and working, Martha failed to just…

> *stop* and enjoy Jesus and
>
> *worship* Him.

And how did Martha's busyness and the neglect of her spiritual life show? You guessed it—she got nervous…fidgety…on edge…cranky. And then she fell apart and lost control. Not only was Martha stomping through her day, but she was stomping through the kitchen, the dining room, and the family room. She even lashed out at her younger sister, Mary. And then (horror of horrors) she lashed out at Jesus!

What Was Wrong?

Martha was definitely out of control. And that led to her saying things she shouldn't have said, to blaming others for her awful condition, to bossing everyone around (even Jesus!), to comparing the amount of work she was doing with the amount of work her sister was (or wasn't!) doing, to complaining, to emoting…. Well, I'm sure you get the picture.

But, what was wrong?

✎ *From God's Word to Your Heart...*

Looking at the Bible's account and what it tells us about both Martha and Mary will answer all our questions. Read it below. It's what I call "the tale of two sisters." And while you're reading, notice what Jesus said was wrong in *Martha's* heart. Notice, too, the words the Bible—and Jesus—uses to describe Martha's conduct. And don't fail to catch how *Mary* is described and what good thing Jesus had to say about her.

> *As Jesus and his disciples were on their way, he came to a village where a woman named Martha opened her home to him. She had a sister called Mary, who sat at the Lord's feet listening to what he said. But Martha was distracted by all the preparations that had to be made. She came to him and asked, "Lord, don't you care that my sister has left me to do the work by myself? Tell her to help me!"*
>
> *"Martha, Martha," the Lord answered, "you are worried and upset about many things, but only one thing is needed. Mary has chosen what is better, and it will not be taken away from her"* (Luke 10:38-42).

What Made the Difference?

As we learn from these two sisters, we mustn't miss the fact that *both* of them loved Jesus (see verses 38-39). Both loved our Lord, and both served Him. But in this scene there was a great difference in their behaviors, which revealed something about what was going on in their hearts at the time.

You see, Mary not only loved serving the Lord, but she loved *listening* to Him. I mean, the split second Jesus started talking, Mary stopped! Her service came to a screeching halt, and she stopped, set her serving dishes aside, and took a seat at Jesus' feet. Why? So she could listen *to* Him—not just do *for* Him! After all, *He* had "the words of eternal life" (John 6:68).

So our dear Mary demonstrated a heart devoted to God by hearing His words and by worshiping Him. She was obsessed with Jesus. My guess is that Mary also loved the quieter disciplines of the Christian life—like sitting down in a favorite place to meditate on Scripture, to pray to God, and maybe even write in a journal or a diary. Whether this is true or not, we do definitely know that Mary knew when and how to make the choice to stop all the busy-ness of life and spend time with God.

And here's another point we don't want to miss. Surely Mary did her work. But Mary made sure her choices gained her the all-important time she needed to take care of her devotion and commitment to God. Yes, hers was a heart devoted to God.

What Is a Heart Devoted to God?

Because Mary was a woman after God's own heart, her heart was devoted to Him. She was preoccupied with one thing at all times—Him! As I said above, Mary was obsessed with the Lord. Therefore Mary consistently made one choice, one decision, that caused Jesus to speak of her as He did. And what was that one choice? Mary chose to spend time hearing God through His Word and worshiping God in her heart. In other words, Mary chose to spend some of her precious time with the Lord.

Time spent in this way, dear one, is the kind of time that is never wasted and can never be taken away from you either (see verse 42). Why? Because it is time spent in eternal pursuits, time that results in both daily and ever-lasting blessings.

Yes, But How?

I know you want to be a woman after God's own heart too, just like Mary was. So *how* can you move in that direction? Consider these three tried-and-true ways.

1. *Choose to spend time with God*—Here's how one woman after God's own heart put it: "I don't want to be robbed of even one of God's riches by not taking time to let Him invade my life. By not listening to what He is telling me. By allowing the routine, pressing matters of my minutes to bankrupt me of time for the most exciting, most fulfilling relationship in life."[1]

Now, how can you make time in your busy day for "the most exciting, most fulfilling relationship in life"? For listening to God? For spending time with Him? For letting Him invade your life?

Listen to what my daughters' high school pastor told their youth group about spending time with God. He asked them, "Would you be willing to go on a bit of a fast each day, a *time* fast? Would you be willing to...

...say *no* to some time watching TV,

...say *no* to some time on the telephone,

...say *no* to some time with friends,

...say *no* to some time in the mall, in order to

...say *yes* to some time with God?"

And now the question is, would *you?*

2. *Choose God's ways at every opportunity*—"In all your ways acknowledge him, and he will make your paths straight" (Proverbs 3:6) could be the theme verse of this entire book—and of life! This well-loved verse describes a two-step partnership with God. *Our part* is to stop and acknowledge God along the way. *God's part* is to direct our paths and make them straight. This means that we are to consult with God regarding our every decision, word, thought, and response. This means that *before* we move ahead or *before* we react to someone or something, we need

to stop and pray first, "God, what would You have me do—or think or say—here?" If you do this you'll find the principles in this poem to be true for you and the choices you make.

> Good, better, best,
> never let it rest
> until your good is better,
> and your better best.

Don't you think this practice of stopping and consulting God *before* acting (and re-acting) like Martha did would help you and me to make the good, better, and best choices in the situations that we confront each day? Don't you think this habit would make us more like Mary?

3. *Commit yourself to God daily*—In Romans 12:1, the apostle Paul says "to offer your bodies as living sacrifices, holy and pleasing to God—this is your spiritual act of worship." As we consider our desire to commit ourselves to God daily, I want you to begin a new practice this week based on Romans 12:1. I want you to begin committing yourself to God daily. And how could you do that? Here's how one man did it. He wrote down a list of what he called "his rules to live by every day." And what was #1 on his list?

> Make a daily, definite, audible dedica-
> tion of yourself to God. Say it out loud—
> "Lord, today I give myself anew to you."[2]

Why not make such a commitment to God daily for
a week? And then why not seek to make it a habit
for life?

4. *Cultivate a hot heart*—God has a few things to say
to us in Revelation 3:15-16 about our heart condition.
Read it for yourself:

> *I know your deeds, that you are neither
> cold nor hot. I wish you were either one
> or the other! So, because you are luke-
> warm—neither hot nor cold—I am
> about to spit you out of my mouth.*

I think it's pretty obvious, according to this scripture,
which heart condition God considers the worst! And
it gets even more serious as we think about these
bone-chilling facts:

- To be *coldhearted* means to be unemotional,
  unconscious of God. Imagine being unemotional about the things of God!

- And to be *lukewarm* means to be indifferent.
  Imagine being indifferent toward God!

- But the third heart temperature is to be yours
  as a woman after God's own heart. You are to

be *hot-hearted*. That means that the heat of your heart and emotion reaches a high temperature. That means boiling over! And such high heat is usually paired up with violent activity, emotion, excitement, and passion. It's fiery! As I said, that's the heart of someone—you!—who's committed to God.

Now, what is your heart's desire…and your heart's temperature toward God?

Heart Response

Are you there, dear one? Is yours the fiery heart of devotion to God that's just been described? Oh, how I pray that it is! But if you're not there, or if you're unsure how to get there, consider these few actions that will most definitely turn up the heat of your heart.

Step One—Do you need to receive Jesus Christ as your personal Savior? This is the beginning step, you know, to becoming a woman after *God's* own heart. Perhaps you need to pray a heartfelt prayer similar to this one:

God, I want to be Your child, a true woman after Your heart—a woman who lives her life in You, and through You, and for You. I acknowledge my sins and shortcomings, my failure to live up to the standards You have set in Your Word, the Bible, and I receive Your Son, Jesus Christ, into my needy heart, giving thanks that He died on the cross for my sins. Thank You for giving me Your grace and Your strength so that I can follow after Your heart.

Step Two—Do you need to be more faithful to set aside time each day to listen to God like Mary did by reading your Bible? By praying? This can and must be a first priority each day. That's how you and I, no matter what our age, make the choice Mary made. That's how we choose the *one* thing, the *good* part, that can never be taken away from us. As we choose to sit at the Lord's feet *regularly*, we cease to act like Martha—too busy, too bossy, too distracted to listen to the Master and linger with Him and delight in Him.

Now, what will *your* choice be today? Tomorrow? Each day? I'm praying for you!

Things to Do Today to Develop a Heart That Is Devoted to God

♡ Think of at least three ways you can make time in your busy day for "the most exciting, most fulfilling relationship in life." How can you ensure time for listening to God, for spending time with Him, for letting Him invade your life?

♡ Memorize the poem below and put it to use in helping you choose God's way in the situations you confront each day.

> Good, better, best,
> never let it rest,
> until your good is better,
> and your better best.

♡ Make a definite, audible dedication of yourself to God today and every day this week.

Would You Like to Know More?
Check It Out

✓ Read Mary and Martha's story in Luke 10:38-42 in your Bible. Describe the scene. Note who was there and what was taking place.

✓ Next, do a character study on Martha. Circle or list the words that describe Martha's conduct. Also note her words—who she spoke to and what she said.

✓ Then do a character study on Mary, noting the words that describe her conduct.

✓ Compare the two sisters. What differences do you notice in their words, actions, attitudes, posture, and interaction with Jesus?

✓ Then ask yourself, Am I busily "serving" Jesus...or sitting at His feet? Am I lashing out at others...or am I listening to my Savior? Am I worrying about life...or am I worshiping the Lord? Am I restless...or am I resting in God? What changes must I make to develop a heart that is devoted to God?

✓ What does Proverbs 31:30 say about the importance of maintaining your relationship with God?

2

A Heart That Loves God's Word

*[You] will be like a tree planted by the water
that sends out its roots by the stream.*

JEREMIAH 17:8

I can still remember the day my husband, Jim, and I planted 13 ivy vines in our backyard with the hopes that these baby plants would one day grow strong enough and full enough to cover our bare and oh-so-ugly(!) cement block walls.

Well, about three months later, my dream was coming true…except for one of the ivy plants. It was absolutely dead! So Jim went to work. He purchased a new replacement plant, got out his shovel, bent over the dead vine, and to his surprise, it slipped right out of the ground. In a glance Jim could see what was wrong. This one plant had failed to grow because there were no roots! Although the plant had enjoyed all the right conditions above ground, something was missing beneath the surface of the soil. It didn't have the root system that is vital for drawing the needed nourishment and moisture from the soil.

What a picture this is for you and me! As women after God's own heart we want to grow in Christ. But, just like any kind of plant, we must take care to nurture a healthy, powerful root system. Our heart's desire is…

> to flourish…not fail
>
> to thrive…not die
>
> to blossom…not wither

Therefore we must devote ourselves to developing a root system that is anchored deep in the Lord and in His Word, the Bible. We must willfully and purposefully spend time in God's Word—reading it, cherishing it, and (most of all) following it. This practice will make all the difference in your life, and in mine, too!

Roots Are Unseen

Where is a thriving root system grown? We know the answer, don't we? It's grown underground. So I want to challenge you to disappear from the public scene for a period of time each day. I want to encourage you to drop out of your friends' sight for a portion of your day. I want to invite you to withdraw from the distractions of TV and the Internet for a time of solitude. Why? So you can tend to your private life, your hidden life, the secret life you enjoy with God. When you and I are faithful to do this one thing each and every day, wow!, what a difference it makes.

But we get it all backwards. We think that the Christian life is made up of people, people, and more people! In fact, it seems like we're always with people—people at home, people at school (and after school), people at church.... On and on the people list goes. Yet, here's the truth:

> The greater the proportion of your day—of your life—spent hidden in quiet, in reflection, in prayer, [in study,] in scheduling, in preparation, the greater will be the effectiveness, the impact, the power of the part of your life that shows.[3]

Roots Are for Taking In

What happens when you and I do slip away to be with God in study and prayer? We receive. We take in. We are nurtured and fed. We ensure our spiritual health and growth. When we spend time with Christ, He supplies us with strength and encourages us in the pursuit of His ways.

I call this time with God "the great exchange." Away from the world and hidden from public view, I exchange...

>   my weariness for His strength,
>
>   my weakness for His power,
>
>   my darkness for His light,
>
>   my problems for His solutions,
>
>   my burdens for His freedom,
>
>   my frustrations for His peace,
>
>   my turmoil for His calm,
>
>   my hopes for His promises,

my afflictions for His balm of comfort,

my questions for His answers,

my confusion for His knowledge,

my doubt for His assurance,

my nothingness for His awesomeness,

the temporal for the eternal, and

the impossible for the possible!

Roots Are for Storage

Roots serve as a reservoir of what we need. As we stop (like Mary did in the previous chapter) and regularly send down our roots into God's Word, into His springs of living water, we begin to collect His life-giving water. Then what happens?

God's Word begins to create in us a reservoir of hope and strength in Him. Then, when times are rough and things get difficult (like when your classmates make fun of your commitment to God...or when you are tempted to give up—or give in to sin...or when a friend turns on you or gossips about you...or when there is tension in the home), you and I won't be depleted. We won't dry up, disintegrate, or die. We won't run out of strength, collapse in exhaustion, or give up.

And here's another wonderful thing that happens. Because of the reservoir, when problems come (and Jesus said they will—see John 16:33!), we can simply reach down into our hidden reservoir of strength and draw out from what God has given us. What's needed is available right at that moment! Like the psalmist wrote about God's people, we will be able to go from "strength to strength" (Psalm 84:7). Yes, roots deep into God's truth are definitely needed when times get rough.

Roots Are for Support

Here's another reason to make sure you spend time in God's Word. Without a well-developed root system, you and I can become top heavy. "Top heavy" is a vivid term used to describe a plant that has lots of leafy, heavy foliage above the ground but nothing to support it from underneath. In other words, there are only a few scanty roots but not enough to hold it up. So, when times get tough (and remember, they will!) and the winds of adversity begin to blow (and they will!), we topple. You see, without a network of strong roots, we have to be staked up, tied up, propped up, and straightened up...until another wind comes along, and over we go again!

Do you want to stand strong in the Lord? Then you must cultivate a strong and healthy root system. Here's what I want for you and me.

> In bygone days a process was used for growing the trees that became the main masts for military and merchant ships. The great shipbuilders first selected a tree located on the top of a high hill as a potential mast. Then they cut away all of the surrounding trees that would shield the chosen one from the force of the wind. As the years went by and the

winds blew fiercely against the tree, the tree only grew stronger until finally it was strong enough to be the foremast of a ship.[4]

✎ *From God's Word to Your Heart...*

Let's pause now and read the verses below. Several describe the characteristics of a plant—or in our case, a woman—whose heart is rooted in God's Word. As you read, be thinking about several things that stand out in your mind and heart from these picturesque verses and the stamina portrayed in each.

> *Blessed is the man who does not walk in the counsel of the wicked or stand in the way of sinners or sit in the seat of mockers. But his delight is in the law of the LORD, and on his law he meditates day and night. He is like a tree planted by streams of water, which yields its fruit in season and whose leaf does not wither. Whatever he does prospers* (Psalm 1:1-3).

> *Blessed is the man who trusts in the LORD, whose confidence is in him. He will be like a tree planted by the water that sends out its*

roots by the stream. It does not fear when heat comes; its leaves are always green. It has no worries in a year of drought and never fails to bear fruit (Jeremiah 17:7-8).

The LORD will guide you always; he will satisfy your needs in a sun-scorched land and will strengthen your frame. You will be like a well-watered garden, like a spring whose waters never fail (Isaiah 58:11).

We are hard pressed on every side, but not crushed; perplexed, but not in despair; persecuted, but not abandoned; struck down, but not destroyed (2 Corinthians 4:8-9).

Yes, But How?

Now, *how* does a woman draw near to God's heart? *How* can you and I put ourselves in a position where God can grow each of us into a woman of remarkable endurance?

1. *Develop the habit of drawing near to God*—Notice the habits of these men of remarkable endurance. Think about what you can learn from each of them.

> Abraham—*Early the next morning Abraham got up and returned to the place where he had stood before the LORD* (Genesis 19:27).

> David—*In the morning, O LORD, you hear my voice; in the morning I lay my requests before you and wait in expectation* (Psalm 5:3).

> Jesus—*Very early in the morning, while it was still dark, Jesus got up, left the house and went off to a solitary place, where he prayed* (Mark 1:35).

> Now for you, my friend. Can you say that your habit of drawing near to God is deeply ingrained? Or is it somewhat regular, merely in-the-making, or needing to be improved?

2. *Design a personal time for drawing near to God*—If you're like most busy women—young or old—your time with the Lord could use a little help. So let's set about to design a better time. (Remember? "Good, better, best....")

When? Did you notice that the three men above had a *time* when they met with God? As you review your daily life and look into your heart, what would be the best time for you? Or put another way, when would you like it to be?

Where? And did you notice that each of these people of God had a *place* for meeting with God? Do you have a place? If not, where would you like your place to be?

What tools? The right tools will make your *time* with God in your *place* more productive, more efficient, and more meaningful. For instance, I take my Bible, my pink highlighter, and my personal journal to my *place* at my *time*. Sometimes I take my favorite devotional book along with me. And sometimes I even use a textbook to look up certain kinds of information (a dictionary, a Bible reference book). Think about how you will stock your *place* so that the next *time* you land there for your devotions, everything you need will be handy.

3. *Detail your daily progress*—One picture is truly worth a thousand words! So I'm asking you to do what I do. Start today to use the chart in the back of your book, "Quiet Times Calendar," to keep track of your all-important devotional life. Simply color in or shade in the days you meet with God and read from His Word. Then a quick glance will tell you how well you're doing in your pursuit of becoming a woman who loves God's Word. (You'll find this chart on pages 218-19.)

Heart Response

Here's something else to think about as you seek to love God's Word even more—if someone asked you to describe the quiet time you had this morning, what would you say?

This is exactly the question Dawson Trotman, founder of The Navigators ministry organization, used to ask young men and women applying for ministry work. In fact, he once spent five days interviewing candidates for overseas missionary service. He spent a half hour with each one, asking specifically about their devotional life. Sadly, only one person out of 29 interviewed said his devotional life was a constant in his life, a source of strength, guidance, and refreshment. As Trotman continued to probe into the lives of those men and women planning a lifetime of service for God, he found that never since they had come to know the Lord had they ever had a consistent devotional life.[5]

Now, my cherished reading friend, how would *your* interview about *your* devotional life go? What answers would *you* be able to give? Ask your heart Mr. Trotman's question now.

And, if your answer isn't all that great, what can you do right this minute to set your life and the pattern of your days in a new direction, a direction that will ensure that you grow in your love for God's Word? After all, as the old saying goes, "Every journey begins with a single step." And that includes your journey to becoming a woman after God's own heart!

Things to Do Today to Develop
a Heart That Loves God's Word

♡ Did you choose a time to be with God yet? If not, do it now. Then pick a place to be alone with God.

♡ List the tools you will need for your place. Then place those tools in your place so that tomorrow you are ready to meet with God.

♡ If you don't know what to study, may I suggest one of the studies in my A Woman After God's Own Heart® Bible Study series? These fun studies were created for busy women (like you!) to be completed in about 15 minutes a day. Every one of them was selected because it focuses on being a woman, on the lives of the women of the Bible, and on our roles as women. You'll find a list of these studies on the last page of this book.

Would You Like to Know More?
Check It Out

✓ Read Psalm 1:1-3. Make a list of the actions of the man or woman whose heart is rooted in God's Word. Note what she does not do and what she does do. What are the results of such a love for God's Word? Are there any changes you must make today?

✓ Do the same for Jeremiah 17:7-8. Here is a picture of spiritual health and growth. Write down the actions of the person who is blessed. Note the hard conditions and the signs of health and strength. Then list the indicators and benefits of spiritual health and growth. Are there any changes you must make today?

✓ Read 2 Corinthians 4:8-9. The apostle Paul was a man after God's own heart who continually drew strength from God when the pressures of life built up. Yet Paul, like the great ship's mast described earlier, stood firm. Because of God's Word, God's truth, God's strength, and God's grace to him, what was Paul able to testify? Are there any changes you must make today to root your heart and life in God's Word so that you can tap into this same kind of strength as you walk through life?

3

A Heart Committed to Prayer

PART 1

*Then Jesus told his disciples a parable
to show them that they should always
pray and not give up.*

LUKE 18:1

I wish I knew more about you, my precious friend! I wish I knew where you live, what your room (and your *place* where you meet with God) looks like, what *you* look like, what your family is like, what some of your favorite things to do might be.

But right this minute, I wish I knew how old you are. Why? Because I made a very important choice in relation to becoming a woman after God's own heart when I was 38 years old, and I'm praying that you are *way* ahead of me in making such a decision! Yes, I'm glad that you're much younger than I was, and I hope you're much further along in your spiritual growth than I was at that time.

Anyway, I made the significant choice on my tenth spiritual birthday. (And, again, I hope you're *way* ahead of me!) On that day I was having my quiet time, my time alone with God. After spending some time thanking Him for His Son and for His salvation of my soul, I dared to turn my thoughts forward. I prayed, "Lord, what do You see missing from my Christian life? What needs attention as I begin a new decade with You?"

Well, before I got the question mark tacked onto my heart-searching prayer, God seemed to respond immediately by calling to my mind an area of great personal struggle and failure—my prayer life!

Oh, I had tried praying. I knew God's Word said I should. But each new effort lasted, at best, only a few days. And then I was back where I started, mumbling something like, "God bless me and my family today." Oh, yes, I had tried praying!

But on that tenth spiritual birthday, I wrote out the following commitment to God:

> I dedicate and purpose to spend the next ten years (Lord willing) developing a meaningful prayer life.

My dear friend, these words, poured out of an earnest heart, launched a complete make-over of my whole life— every part and person and pursuit in it! And I want to share with you just a few of the blessings of prayer that became mine. And take heart! They're blessings that can become yours as well.

Blessing #1: A Deeper Relationship with God

When you and I spend regular, daily, unhurried time in prayer with God, we experience a deeper relationship with Him. And we grow spiritually in a multitude of ways. Here are just a few examples.

Prayer increases faith—I had heard that a good way to grow in faith in God was to keep a prayer list. And so I began to write out a prayer list. With my list in hand, I began taking my concerns for family, friends, and myself to God each day. I was awed as, for the first time ever, I paid close attention to how He answered item after item! And, of course, with each day, each prayer time, and each answer, my faith in God grew.

Prayer provides a place to unload burdens—What is your #1 problem today? And what are the other pressing problems of your life? Today, right now in fact, one of my best friends is having cancer surgery. I am a thousand miles away, unable to be with her or help in any way. My heart is heavy and anxious! But through prayer I am doing what the Bible tells you and me to do—I am "casting" my problem and my burden on my heavenly Father (1 Peter 5:7). I know when I do this, when I do what God says to do with the cares of my life and the cares of my friend's life, I'm putting my impossible problems into His able hands. God will take care of them...as only He can.

When you and I begin each day by giving all the cares of life to God in prayer, we can then rise up relieved, freed from many heavy weights. Author and fellow pray-er Corrie ten Boom offers a vivid image of this privilege. She writes,

As a camel kneels before his
master to have him remove his
burden, so kneel and let the
Master take your burden.[6]

I also like this advice given by a poet in a scene
between the Lord and one of His children. I don't know
who wrote it, but it says it all!

But this you must remember,
This one thing you must know...
I cannot take your burden
Until you let it go.

Prayer teaches us that God is always near—What can
you do when trouble strikes? I mean trouble like a tragedy,
a catastrophe, a disaster? Well, my friend, I had the opportunity to find out on January 17, 1994, at 4:31 in the
morning, when a devastating 6.8 killer earthquake struck
our home in California. I was home alone and can only
remember trying to save my life by getting out of the
house. And, as I cried out to God while staggering toward
the front door, with our house literally buckling and
cracking beneath my bare feet, from the depths of my heart
and soul came God's reassurance of His presence. And it
came from a passage out of the Bible (Psalm 46:1-2) that
I had planted there by memorizing it.

God is our refuge and strength,
an ever-present help in trouble.
Therefore we will not fear...

(And, by the way, the rest of this passage and the next verse just happens to go like this: "...though the earth give way and the mountains fall into the heart of the sea, though its waters roar and foam and the mountains quake with their surging"! Sounds like an earthquake to me!)

Beloved young sister, the more you and I pray, the more we are reminded of God's powerful presence in time of need! One man put it this way: "The purpose of prayer is to reveal the presence of God equally present all the time in every condition."[7]

Prayer trains us not to panic—Jesus said we shouldn't give up, give in, or panic. No, He said we should pray instead (see Luke 18:1). In other words, we are not to give in, cave in, or collapse under pressure. Instead we are to persevere. Turning to God for every need during your regular daily prayer time will ingrain in you the habit of prayer, which can then replace your natural tendency to panic at the first hint of any problem.

Prayer changes lives—You've probably heard that "prayer changes *things*." But, dear one, once you develop a more regular prayer life you'll discover that "prayer changes *you*"!

✎ *From God's Word to Your Heart...*

Wow! Look at all the ways you and I grow in our trust in God and in our knowledge of God when we pray! What good news! But now I want you to see for yourself what

God has to say about enjoying a deeper relationship with Him through prayer. Interact with these teachings from the Bible. Note the instructions they give you…right from God's Word to your heart. And while you're at it, think about something you can do to put these powerful truths and promises into action concerning the issues of your life today, tomorrow, and all your future tomorrows.

> *Then Jesus told his disciples a parable to show them that they should always pray and not give up* (Luke 18:1).

> *Cast all your anxiety on him because he cares for you* (1 Peter 5:7).

> *God is our refuge and strength, an ever-present help in trouble. Therefore we will not fear* (Psalm 46:1-2).

> *I lift up my eyes to the hills—where does my help come from? My help comes from the LORD, the Maker of heaven and earth* (Psalm 121:1-2).

Call to me and I will answer you and tell you great and unsearchable things you do not know (Jeremiah 33:3).

Thanks for taking the time to look at the verses above. I hope (and pray!) these scriptures gave you a better idea of what I've been saying about the blessing of a deeper relationship with God through prayer. We are indeed blessed to enjoy the privilege of prayer, of conversing with almighty God. May your heart be encouraged to pray. And may your prayers be ever lifted to our great God so that...

you are growing in faith,

you are handing off your burdens,

you are more aware of the presence of God,

you are less likely to panic when troubles arise, and

you are being changed and transformed into the image of God's dear Son and your Savior, Jesus Christ!

Heart Response

I know we took a long time on this one blessing (a whole chapter, in fact!). But wasn't it eye-opening to drink in just these few ways that the one discipline of praying daily can help us to grow spiritually? And don't you agree that your relationship with God is vitally important? After all, you, like me, desire to be a woman after *His* heart. And it's truly incredible and unbelievable that you and I can enjoy a relationship with the God of the universe! It's truly by His grace!

So now, dear heart, I am inviting you to make a commitment similar to the one I made. And while you're at it, thank God profusely that you're not 38 years old like I was when I made my commitment! That means you have a 20- to 25-year head start on me. I'm deliriously happy for you!

And I have more good news for you. When I decided to learn more about the awesome privilege of prayer, I fully expected drudgery and joyless labor. But as I moved ahead on my commitment to develop a meaningful prayer life, I was surprised by the blessings that began to blossom in my heart. As a favorite hymn tells us, "Count your blessings, name them one by one." And dear one, as I said, these are just a few!

Now, write out your own personal commitment to develop your prayer life. Then let's look in our next chapter at even more blessings that come our way as we pray.

My Commitment to Pray

_____
_____
_____
_____
_____
_____
_____
_____
_____
_____
_____
_____
_____
_____
_____
_____
_____
_____
_____
_____
_____
_____

Things to Do Today to Develop a Heart Committed to Prayer

♡ Did you make your personal commitment to prayer? If not, why not? It's not too late to do it. Just remember that *desire* is half the victory, and your prayer of commitment is an expression of your desire to become a woman of prayer.

♡ Now that you've made that commitment (you did make it, right?), take a sheet of paper—maybe a page in your personal notebook or planner—and list the people you want to pray for. The next time you pray, read each person's name aloud to God. Then say what's on your heart about each dear person. Keep moving right on through your list as time permits.

♡ Begin another prayer list of your own personal concerns—your #1 problem, some decision you must make, some behavior you should change, some fear that tends to rob you of your joy in the Lord. Then pray...instead of giving in to these pressures.

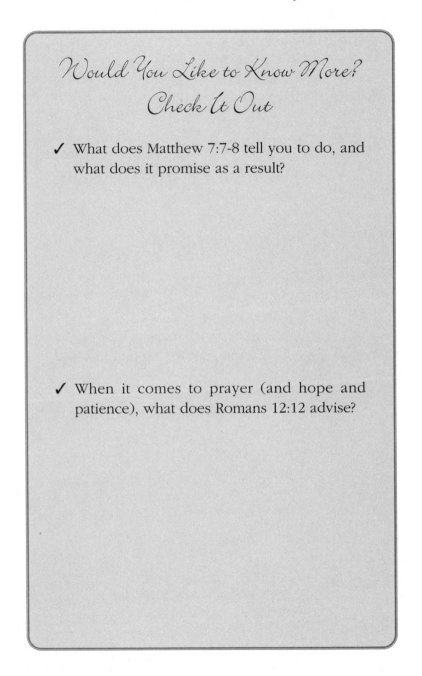

Would You Like to Know More?
Check It Out

✓ What does Matthew 7:7-8 tell you to do, and what does it promise as a result?

✓ When it comes to prayer (and hope and patience), what does Romans 12:12 advise?

✓ How can you have peace and live a life that is free from anxiety, according to Philippians 4:6-7?

✓ How faithful should Christians—and you—be in the area of prayer, according to Colossians 4:2?

✓ For the recipe to a wonderful life, see 1 Thessalonians 5:16-18!

✓ What does Hebrews 4:16 say your attitude should be as you pray...and what are the blessed results?

✓ In case you are hesitant to pray, what assurance is noted in 1 Peter 3:12?

4

A Heart Committed to Prayer

PART 2

*The prayer of a righteous man
is powerful and effective.*

JAMES 5:16

Even though we've never met, I have *so* enjoyed praying for you, my unseen friend! Do you realize what an amazing person you are? That *you* hold the keys to the future of Christianity (humanly speaking, that is)? That you are one of the significant godly young women of today who will become the godly women (and possibly wives and mothers) of the years to come? And I know that you care about your spiritual growth because you've chosen to work your way through a book like this one. Oh, how I thank God for *you*. And I thank Him that you truly desire a close relationship with Him.

There's a young woman in the Bible who reminds me of you. She's Mary, who became the mother of our Lord Jesus Christ. Maybe you already know that Mary was about 14 years old when God sent His angel Gabriel to speak to her (Luke 1:26-38). What do we know about Mary at that point in her life? We know that...

> she was completely committed to God's will for her life (verse 38).
>
> she was highly favored by God (verses 28 and 30).
>
> she was a virgin (verses 27 and 34).

One thing I really love about Mary is her prayer life. In fact, her prayer life was so stunning that God has used Mary—a 14-year-old, a teenager!—to teach all Christian women down through the centuries how to pray. You see, Mary truly had that deeper relationship with God that we talked about in our last chapter. And surely that relationship was partly developed as she prayed to her heavenly Father. You and I can learn much about prayer by reading what is called "Mary's Magnificat" or "The Song of Mary" in Luke 1:46-55. The first thing that impresses us in Mary's Song is that when Mary opened her mouth to pray, the first words that rushed forth were, "My soul glorifies the Lord and my spirit rejoices in God my Savior" (verses 46-47).

And now it's our turn, dear one. It's time for us to learn more about prayer and about how to further develop a heart that is committed to prayer. To review, we've already discussed that Blessing #1 is a deeper relationship with God. Now let's go on and look at even more of the blessings that are ours through prayer.

Blessing #2: Greater Purity

In our last chapter I mentioned that prayer changes us. And now I want to point out that one major change prayer brings about in us is greater purity. Becoming more like Christ is a process of spiritual growth that requires dealing with sin. And taking the confession of sin seriously during prayer time moves that process along, causing us to purge our life of practices that are not pleasing to God.

I certainly know this to be true in my life. How? Because I was able to pinpoint a serious sin area in my daily life, a habit that I *knew* went against God's Word. In both 1 Timothy 3:11 and Titus 2:3, God says—in black and white!—that His women are not to gossip. And (you guessed it!) I had a terrible problem with gossip.

But there's good news, too! Real change began when I started to not only pray about gossip, but to confess it as sin each time I did it. I began to acknowledge to God (and admit to myself!) that this practice went against His Word, that it was harmful to His people and to others, and that it had no place in my life as a child of God. Now, don't get me wrong—I still have my struggles. But believe me when I tell you that I am not the same gossiping woman I used to be! Purification—purging my life of a major sin—took place, in part, because I faced my sin regularly in prayer. In other words, the conviction of sin led to confession...which led to purging...which led to greater purity.

From God's Word to Your Heart...

Now that I've told you a little about one of my problem areas, let's see what God's Word says about purifying ourselves of practices that are not pleasing to Him. Note what this verse teaches us as women after God's own heart about greater purity.

> *If we confess our sins, he is faithful and just and will forgive us our sins and purify us from all unrighteousness* (1 John 1:9).

Now, do what I did (and still do). Pinpoint one practice in your life that you know is not pleasing to God, a practice or habit that is, in fact, directly opposed to His Word. Put that sinful action at the top of your prayer list. Then pray about it—every day. (Pray about it every *minute* of every day, if you have to!) And confess it to God when you fail. Ask God to help you create a plan of action to radically remove it from your life. Be severe! Be decisive! Be whatever you must be and do whatever you must do to move toward purifying yourself of this one area. It'll be tough, but cry out to God for His help and for His grace to do battle and to get a grip on this area of your life. A woman after God's own heart willingly sacrifices her favorite sins for greater purity!

Blessing #3: Confidence in Making Decisions

How do you make decisions? If you're like most women, you make them based on how you *feel* at the moment some opportunity comes along. In other words, you make *physical* decisions and *emotional* decisions—not *spiritual* decisions. You tend to make decisions that are based on your physical and/or emotional state at the moment rather than waiting to make decisions that are spiritually made through—and after—prayer.

Well, dear one, I just described me! Here's a typical scenario from my life (before I began to pray about my choices). If some opportunity came up, and I was tired at the moment, guess what my answer was? *No!* Or if I felt frayed and frazzled around the edges, like I just couldn't handle one more thing, again, my answer was *no!*

But I learned to follow a three-step pattern that has helped me make better decisions. (Remember? "Good, better, best....") I learned to...

1) *wait* to make decisions so that I could

2) *write* them down on my prayer list and then

3) *wait* on God for direction.

As a result, I came up with this prayer principle for my decision making (which I gladly pass on to you!):

~ *No decision made without prayer!* ~

✎ *From God's Word to Your Heart...*

We want to be women after God's own heart, right? So let's note what these scriptures teach us about the lives and hearts of two of God's devoted servants.

Hear God's report of King David's heart—*After removing Saul, [God] made David their king. He testified concerning him: "I have found David son of Jesse a man after my own heart; he will do everything I want him to do"* (Acts 13:22).

Hear the heart cry of the apostle Paul—*"What shall I do, Lord?"* (Acts 22:10).

Now, how do you think 1) *waiting* before you make a decision so that you have time to 2) *write* down the decision(s) you must make and then 3) *waiting* on God's direction through prayer would help you make good, better, and best decisions? And how do you think the prayer principle *no decision made without prayer* would help?

Blessing #4: Improved Relationships

What a blessing prayer is! Prayer results in better relationships with people—*all* people! How can this be? Because as you pray for others, you find these prayer principles to be true.

- *You cannot think about yourself and others at the same time.* (Praying for others forces you to think of others.)

- *You cannot hate the person you are praying for.* (Prayer is an act of love that changes your heart.)

- *You cannot neglect the person you are praying for.* (Prayer causes you to care more about others as you carry them in your heart.)

✎ *From God's Word to Your Heart...*

While we're thinking about our prayer life, let's touch on friendships and relationships for a minute or two. I know that every teen struggles with friends—with making and maintaining friendships. As a Christian woman I know you want healthy personal relationships. And that includes your relationships with your parents and brothers and sisters. Plus we all have relationships to nurture beyond the family circle, relationships with not only our best friends but also with those who are unkind. And then there are "boy" friends!

But as we pray about these relationships—about all our relationships—we witness many improvements. Here's a list of the major categories of relationships that probably fill your life. Note what the Bible says about them and how you can pray accordingly.

Parents

Children, obey your parents in the Lord, for this is right. "Honor your father and mother"—which is the first commandment with a promise—"that it may go well with you and that you may enjoy long life on the earth" (Ephesians 6:1-3). *Children, obey your parents in everything, for this pleases the Lord* (Colossians 3:20).

Friends

Do not be misled: "Bad company corrupts good character" (1 Corinthians 15:33). *A man of many companions may come to ruin, but there is a friend who sticks closer than a brother* (Proverbs 18:24).

Boyfriends

An unmarried woman or virgin is concerned about the Lord's affairs: Her aim is to be devoted to the Lord in both body and spirit (1 Corinthians 7:34). *It is God's will that you should...avoid sexual immorality; that each of you should learn to control his own body in a way that is holy and honorable.... For God did not call us to be impure, but to live a holy life* (1 Thessalonians 4:3-4,7).

Enemies

Love your enemies, do good to those who hate you, bless those who curse you, pray for those who mistreat you (Luke 6:27-28).

Whether we are praying for our loved ones, our friends, or our unloved ones(!), a heart that is committed to pray for others makes a difference in those relationships. I once heard about a teacher who assigned her students the following project: They were to select the person on campus they disliked the most. Daily during the coming month, they were to pray for that person and then go out of their way to do some act of kindness for that person. Here's what one young woman wrote after the month was up:

> By the end of the month my dislike of [the girl selected] had been replaced by a growing compassion and understanding....[This assignment] helped me see things about myself—my unfriendliness, my lack of compassion, my

judging without first trying to understand the causes of behavior I disliked.

Let's ask God to help us have greater love and compassion for others. Let's pray for others.

Blessing #5: Contentment

Oh, wow, is this ever an area for prayer! Why is it that we are rarely satisfied? That we worry about our lives? That it seems like everyone else has what we want? That we're on the slow track to popularity, achievement, development, relationships, growth? The list of our discouragements could truly go on and on!

Well, thank the Lord that contentment is ours...when we pray! Before we dive into what God tells us about how to grow in contentment, think a minute about the things you worry about. If you want to, jot them down here.

✎ *From God's Word to Your Heart...*

Now let's see how God's guidelines for contentment can help you and me not to worry.

> *Do not worry about tomorrow* (Matthew 6:34).
> *Do not be anxious about anything, but in everything, by prayer and petition, with*

*thanksgiving, present your requests to God.
And the peace of God, which transcends all
understanding, will guard your hearts and
your minds in Christ Jesus* (Philippians 4:6-7).
*I have learned to be content whatever the cir-
cumstances....I have learned the secret of
being content in any and every situation....I
can do everything through him who gives me
strength* (Philippians 4:11-13).

Look at your own list of "worries." How will you put
these principles to work the next time you worry?

Yes, But How?

I know we've covered a lot in this chapter! And I don't
want to leave you without giving you some very practical
ways to get started on your commitment to pray.

1. Start a prayer log to record requests and responses
   as you travel your own personal journey of prayer.

2. Set aside time each day to linger with the Lord in
   prayer and remember that *something is better than
   nothing.* Begin small—and watch for the mighty
   effects!

3. Pray always (Ephesians 6:18) and in all places, enjoying God's presence with you wherever you go (Joshua 1:9).

4. Pray faithfully for others, especially your parents and brothers and sisters. And don't forget to pray for your enemies (Luke 6:28)!

5. Take seriously the powerful privilege of prayer.

When it comes to my prayer life, I have a saying that helps me each day—*First things first*. I try to make my quiet time with God the first thing I do each morning. Somehow, dedicating my fresh new day to God in prayer first thing makes a tremendous difference in that day. It reminds me who I am (His child) and who I am to serve (Him!) and what I am to do with my day…and my life (glorify Him). And as I pray for the people in my life, the very act of prayer amazingly changes my heart toward them as God gives me His love and His wisdom for living out these relationships in a way that causes Christ to shine through me.

And now I have a question for you: Do you think praying—even for just five or ten minutes a day—could change your life? I believe it can! Lingering in God's presence will increase your faith, provide a place for you to unload your burdens, remind you that God is always near, and help you not to panic when troubles come. When you accept God's invitation to pray, He will transform your heart and change your life.

Now *that's* exciting! All this…and more!…is available to you, my friend, as you nurture a heart committed to prayer. What will your first step be?

Things to Do Today to Develop a Heart Committed to Prayer

♡ Make a prayer sheet for each member of your family and begin praying daily for them. Ask each family member what needs you can pray for.

♡ Begin a prayer sheet for listing the decisions you must make. Be faithful to bring them to God in prayer each day. Ask Him for His wisdom.

♡ Pick out the person you dislike the most and pray daily for her or him for one month.

Would You Like to Know More?
Check It Out

✓ In Luke 1:46-55, Mary pours out her heart in prayer. Write out how Mary referred to herself, and how she referred to God. List, too, her descriptions of God. What strikes you most about her prayer? What ingredients of her prayer can you include in yours?

✓ What do you learn about Jesus' prayers in Mark 1:35? What ingredients of His prayer life can you include in yours?

✓ What is said about Elijah and his prayer life in James 5:17-18? What ingredients of His prayer life can you include in yours? (Notice what James 5:16 says—"The prayer of a righteous man [or woman!] is powerful and effective.")

5

A Heart That Obeys

I have found David...a man after my own heart;
he will do everything I want him to do.

ACTS 13:22

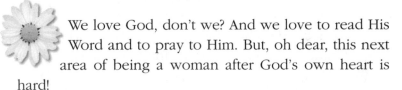We love God, don't we? And we love to read His Word and to pray to Him. But, oh dear, this next area of being a woman after God's own heart is hard!

I'm talking about obedience. And I can never think about the importance of obedience to God without remembering an evening when my daughter Katherine made brownies for the rest of the family...and left out the salt. Well, you know the results! We had to throw out the whole batch because an all-important something was missing and they tasted awful.

And beloved, just as a batch of brownies requires several ingredients to become what we intend it to be, several ingredients are key to our becoming women after God's own heart. We've already talked about devotion to God, devotion to His Word, and devotion to prayer. But one more ingredient—as important as salt in brownies—goes into making you and me women after God's own heart, and that ingredient is obedience. The heart God delights in is a heart that is teachable, willing, and responsive to Him and His commands. In short, it's a heart that obeys.

Two Kinds of Hearts

Just how did I come up with the title of this book, *A Young Woman After God's Own Heart?* Well, it's drawn from the Bible, from Acts 13:22. It's from a sermon preached by the apostle Paul. And in that sermon, Paul pointed out the lives of two different men who had two kinds of hearts. Here's what we know about these two men.

> *King Saul*—The first man was Saul, who reigned as king over Israel and God's people for 40 years.
>
> - Saul served himself and did things his way.
>
> - Saul's worship consisted of outward acts of sacrifice only.
>
> - Saul's heart was centered on Saul.
>
> - Saul's devotion to God was impulsive and irregular.
>
> - Saul was proud and relied on his own skill, his own wisdom and judgment, and his own physical strength.

King David—The second man was David, who served as king over God's people after God removed Saul as king.

- David's heart was willing to obey God.

- David served God, not himself.

- David was concerned with following God's will, not his own.

- David's heart was centered on God, not on himself.

- David, a mighty warrior, depended upon God for his victories and repeatedly declared, "The LORD is the stronghold of my life" (Psalm 27:1).

God gave both these kings opportunities to lead Israel, but in the end they walked down different paths—Saul away from God and David toward Him. These two men were like two different musicians, one who sits down at a piano and plunks on it, here a little, there a little (everyone can play "Chopsticks"!) and the other who sits for hours at a time, a disciplined, faithful, and dedicated student. The first creates immature, irregular, crude sounds that fade away, while the other learns, grows, excels, and lifts the hearts and souls of others as he fine-tunes his music—his life—to the Almighty. Saul's song—his walk with the Lord— was fickle, on again, off again, and undeveloped. But David, known as the sweet psalmist of Israel (2 Samuel 23:1 KJV), offered up to God pure melodies of devoted love and heartfelt obedience. Truly, his was a heart after God!

Now it's your turn to look at what God's Word has to say about these two men and their two kinds of hearts. As you read these verses, look into the mirror of God's Word and ask God and yourself, "Is mine a heart of obedience?"

As you read these verses, note the two men mentioned, what is said about each, and how God defines a man after His own heart.

> *"The LORD has sought out a man after his own heart and appointed him leader of his people, because you have not kept the LORD's command"* (1 Samuel 13:14).

> *After removing Saul, [God] made David their king. He testified concerning him: "I have found David son of Jesse a man after my own heart; he will do everything I want him to do"* (Acts 13:22).

As we've learned here, Saul was a man who simply did not care to obey God! He was not a man after God's own heart...and David was!

Yes, But How?

But more important to me than Saul's heart and David's heart is *your* heart! I think I can safely say that you wouldn't be reading this book if you didn't want to follow after God's own heart by faithfully following His Word and His will. So the question now becomes, *how?* How can we follow David's example in our devotion to God? And what can we do so that God can grow in us a heart that is committed to obedience? A heart committed to doing God's will is an important ingredient when it comes to living out our love for God.

Well, dear one, God calls us to take care of our hearts. God tells you and me to "guard" our hearts with all diligence, for it affects everything we do. He tells us to mark out the path of our feet, to look straight ahead, and not get sidetracked. Rather than turning to the right or to the left, we are to follow the ways that are established by God (see Proverbs 4:23-27).

And what is the key here? Answer: The key to living a life of obedience—a life that stays on God's path—is the heart. If we guard our hearts, if we diligently attend to them, then all the issues, the actions, the "on-goings and the out-goings" of life will be handled God's way.[8]

So how can you and I stay on God's path? Here are several proven guidelines—Five C's—for nurturing a heart that is responsive to God and His ways. These five guidelines, precious one, will help lead us to a life of obedience.

Five Guidelines to Obedience

1. *Concentrate on doing what is right*—When God looked into David's heart, He saw there what He wants to see in you and me, too. He saw a heart that will do His will. And that calls for a tender and teachable heart, a heart that will concentrate on doing what is right.

Many times we know exactly what the right thing to do is, don't we? But what about those times when we're unsure? I mean those times when, in your heart, you want to do the right thing, but you're just not sure what that right thing is? Well, take heart! Here are a few rules to live by when this happens to you.

- Don't do anything! To do what is right, you must take time to pray, ask God for guidance, think, search the Scriptures, and ask advice from someone more mature in Christ. Simply say to the person who is asking you to do something you're unsure of, "I'm going to have to give this some thought. I'll let you know later." Your best plan of action is to do nothing until you know what the right thing to do is. As Proverbs 3:5 instructs, "lean not on your own understanding"!

- Do acknowledge God. Instead of leaning on your own understanding, "in all your ways acknowledge him." Then what happens? "He will make your paths straight" (Proverbs 3:6).

- Do ask for wisdom. Again, the Bible is clear when it instructs that "if any of you lacks wisdom, he should ask God...and it will be given to him" (James 1:5).

- Again, don't do anything. The bottom line for you and me as women after God's own heart is this—when in doubt, *don't* (Romans 14:23)! Or, put another way, *when in doubt, it's out.*

2. *Cease doing what is wrong*—The split second you think or do anything contrary to God's heart, stop immediately! Just put the skids on the activity. If it's gossip, stop. If it's an unworthy thought, stop (Philippians 4:8). If there's a spark of anger in your heart, stop before you act on it. If you've spoken an unkind word, stop before you speak another.

3. *Confess any wrong*—When it comes to this principle from Scripture, I deal very bluntly with myself. When I do something against God's Word, I acknowledge in my heart that what I did is wrong. I say, "This is wrong! This is sin! I can't do this!" After all, as the Bible says, "if we claim to be without sin, we deceive ourselves" (1 John 1:8). So I call sin "sin," and by doing this I am actively training my heart to be responsive to God's convicting Spirit. So, you and I must...

- Confess sin (1 John 1:9), and the sooner the better!

- Forsake sin. God's Word calls us to confess *and* forsake our sins (Proverbs 28:13). Don't be like the farmer who said, "I want to confess that I stole some hay from my neighbor." When the clergyman asked, "How much did you steal?" The farmer declared, "I stole half a load, but make it a whole load. I'm going back to get the other half tonight!"

4. *Clear things up with others*—It's true that confession makes things right with God. But what if you've hurt another person? Then, my fine young friend, you must clear things up with that person, too.

   That's just what I had to do on the very first morning I sang in our church choir. As I walked into the choir room early that morning, a sweet, friendly woman stuck her hand out, smiled, and said, "Hey, are you one of the new guys?" I snapped back, "No, but I'm one of the new *girls*." Well, I knew immediately what I had to do. I took care of the sin of unkindness and cruel speech with God by a prayer in my heart. (And believe me, that was the easy part!) But...I had hurt a person! And she was one of God's precious children! So after the choir finished singing, I waited for this dear woman, stuck out my hand, and said, "I really have a smart mouth, don't I? I'm sorry I responded to your kindness with such a smart remark! Will you please forgive me?"

   God doesn't want us to offer anything to Him until we've made things right with our brothers and sisters. Then, *after* we've settled matters with others, we may come and offer Him our gift of worship (see Matthew 5:23-24).

5. *Continue on as soon as possible*—Have you ever done something wrong, confessed it to God, stopped

doing it, even made things right with others involved, but you just couldn't get over it? I call this behavior "wallowing." I mean, it's over…but I just can't seem to go on because I keep wallowing in what I did. I keep right on reliving my failure. I say to myself, "I can't believe you did that, said that, thought that, acted like that! How could you have done that? You're unworthy! You're totally unfit to serve God."

Well, whenever you and I play out this scene, we need to turn to another truth from God's Word and let it lift us up, dust us off, refresh us, and set us back on His path. God's Word directs us to stop wallowing and to be "forgetting what is behind" so that we can spend our energy "straining toward what is ahead" (Philippians 3:13-14). It's true that we must remember the lessons learned through failure. But it's also true that we must not fail to go on.

From God's Word to Your Heart…

We've certainly covered a lot of ground in this lesson—important ground! But I don't want us to leave this section without seeing and handling the Scriptures ourselves. So I want you to read these powerful truths for yourself. They are truths that deal with cultivating a heart that obeys.

And as you're reading, notice what each of these Bible passages teaches you about living a life of obedience—a life that stays on God's path. What advice does each one give that would help you to live a life of obedience? And, if you're really brave, make note of any changes you need to make so that yours is a heart that obeys.

> *If any of you lacks wisdom, he should ask God, who gives generously to all without finding fault, and it will be given to him* (James 1:5).

> *If we claim to be without sin, we deceive ourselves and the truth is not in us. If we confess our sins, he is faithful and just and will forgive us our sins and purify us from all unrighteousness* (1 John 1:8-9).

> *He who conceals his sins does not prosper, but whoever confesses and renounces them finds mercy* (Proverbs 28:13).

> *But one thing I do: Forgetting what is behind and straining toward what is ahead, I press on toward the goal to win the prize for which God has called me heavenward in Christ Jesus* (Philippians 3:13-14).

Heart Response

Well, precious one, as we step out on the path to becoming a woman after God's own heart, it's obvious that obedience is a foundational stepping-stone on that path. And I know you'll want sure footing here. And such a step—the step of obedience—will prepare you to respond later to what God has to say about the other important areas of your life. So I have a few questions for you.

In Saul's day, God declared that He was looking for a heart that would obey Him, that would do all His will. Do these words describe your heart? Is God's desire your desire? Does your heart follow hard after God (Psalm 63:8 KJV), close to Him, on His heels, literally clinging to Him?[9]

If not, then I beg you to stop right now. Search your heart. Pinpoint any behavior that calls for a heart response of confession. Then make the confession, choose to cast off that behavior, and step right back onto God's path of beauty, peace, and joy, the path enjoyed by a woman after God's own heart, whatever her age. As you desire all that God desires, love all that He loves, and humble yourself under His mighty hand (1 Peter 5:6), then your heart will indeed be a heart after God. What a blessed thought!

Now, my precious friend, how's the recipe of your heart? Is anything missing? Any key ingredient like, say... obedience? Is yours a heart that obeys? A favorite line of poetry prompts you and me, "Little one, search that heart of thine." I'm searching mine. How about you?

Things to Do Today to Develop a Heart That Obeys

♡ Write out the "Five Guidelines to Obedience" on a 3" x 5" card. Over the next several days memorize them.

♡ List any issues where you are struggling with doing what is right. *Lay* your issues next to the guidelines, *pray*, and *obey* God's instructions.

♡ Do you need help with any of the guidelines? Don't turn the page until you've asked someone to help you do everything God wants you to do (Acts 13:22).

Would You Like to Know More?
Check It Out

✓ Read Proverbs 4:23-27. Write down the references to the human body and God's instructions regarding each member of the body mentioned. What we love and what we do make all the difference in the world in how we live. Ask yourself, "Are the things I love leading me in the right direction—in God's direction?"

✓ Make a list of the principles taught in Proverbs 3:5-6 that can help you do what is right. Do the same with Psalm 37:3-5 and Psalm 1:1-2. Go a step further and make two columns— "What to do" and "What not to do," listing God's instructions under the appropriate column. Once again, are the things you love leading you in the right direction, on the path of obedience?

✓ See now what God says about our relationships with others in Matthew 5:23-24. How important are right relationships when it comes to your worship of God? What does God say to do about a broken relationship? What is on God's "to-do" list when it comes to our relationships with others and our relationship with Him?

Part Two

The Pursuit of God's Priorities

6

A Heart That Submits

PART 1

Children, obey your parents in everything, for this pleases the Lord.

COLOSSIANS 3:20

Whenever I'm asked to name the books I've read that have been the most life-changing for me, I always include *What Is a Family?* by Edith Schaeffer.[10] In fact, I've read it more than once...even more than twice. Through her wonderful writing and out of her large heart, the woman who wrote this lovely book was able to paint a picture of what God must have meant family life to be. I know my family life hardly measured up! And that may be true of yours, too.

But I want us to know what the Bible says about the individual roles of each member of the family circle. After all, we all live in families! And we all have parents. Plus most of us have a brother or sister...or two! So let's start with these core relationships and learn how to nurture a heart that submits when it comes to family.

Honoring Your Parents

You've probably heard of the Ten Commandments that Moses brought down from Mount Sinai. They were spoken by God to Moses, who delivered them to God's people. They were (and still are!) God's guidelines for how He wanted His people to live. They weren't God's Ten *Suggestions*. No, they were God's Ten *Commandments*, the law of God. And one of those commandments states this:

> *Honor your father and your mother, so that you may live long in the land the* LORD *your God is giving you* (Exodus 20:12).

My friend, as one writer exclaimed, this commandment regarding our attitude toward our parents is "a BIGGIE in the Bible"![11] Why? Because it's found in the Ten Commandments.

So what's a young woman after God's heart to do about this command? Well, as we learned in our previous chapter, we are to obey it. That's what a woman after God's own heart does. Remember? She fulfills all God's Word, keeps His commandments, and does everything He wants her to do. So, dear heart, you and I are going to honor our fathers and our mothers…as long as they are alive. This applies to you at your age. And it applies to me at my age (my mother just happens to be 93!). It's one of God's forever commandments.

Our next question has got to be, "What then does it mean to honor your parents?" I like this explanation. It may appear simplistic, but I think it covers about everything …including our "Yes, buts" and our "But, what ifs."

> What does it mean to "honor" parents? Partly, "honoring" means speaking well of them and politely to them. It also means acting in a way that shows them courtesy and respect (but we are not to follow them in acts of disobedience to God). Parents have a special place in God's sight. Even those who find it difficult to get along with their parents are still commanded to honor them.[12]

Therefore, to obey God's commandment to honor your parents, you also need to obey your parents (except, as the statement above says, if they are asking you to sin against God). Such obedience calls for you to have a humble heart (1 Peter 5:5). I also think a better understanding of a few other teachings will assist you in your obedience. For instance, did you know that...

- Parents are commanded by God to teach their children (Deuteronomy 6:7)?

- Parents are commanded by God to train their children (Ephesians 6:4)?

- Parents are commanded by God to discipline and correct their children (Hebrews 12:7)?

I can tell you from experience that the hardest thing I've ever had to do as a woman after God's own heart was to follow through on God's command to me, as a young mom, to discipline my two little ones. And I suspect every other young mom has the same struggle! But I knew the Bible said that if I loved my darlings, I would discipline them (Proverbs 13:24). You see, when parents discipline their children, it proves their love. I'm sure I did it wrong a few times (maybe more!). But the Bible says when a child is left to himself, that child is not loved and will ultimately become a heartache to his or her parents (Proverbs 29:15). Therefore, with the encouragement of the Scriptures, with much prayer, and with many tears, I disciplined my children. (And now it's their turn with their five little ones!)

So why am I talking about mothering in a book written to you and your teenage friends who are not yet mothers? For two reasons. First, I want to let you know what God says to parents—*your* parents. And second, I want you to know how hard it is for parents to obey God. And it's hard, too, to be sure you are disciplining properly. But the bottom line is that if parents don't discipline, then there's a real mess to deal with later! Read on and see for yourself!

✎ *From God's Word to Your Heart...*

Meet Eli and his two sons. Eli was one of God's high priests who judged Israel. And, believe me, his story is a sad one! Why? Because he failed to discipline his sons. Rather than wholeheartedly taking on the God-ordered responsibility of a parent to correct his children when they sin, Eli did little or nothing. He let his sons get away with "murder"! Not literally, but his sons did take the best of the burnt animal offerings that the people gave to God and kept the meat for their own food. They were also guilty of blaspheming God and "slept with the women who served at the entrance to the Tent of Meeting" where the worship of God took place (1 Samuel 2:22).

We don't know what led up to Eli's failure in his important role as parent to his sons. The Bible doesn't say. Maybe he tried to discipline and correct his boys in their early years. Maybe he tried a few times with little or no results and then just gave up. Or maybe he tried and his sons refused to cooperate. Or maybe he just didn't take the time. Perhaps he just didn't want to be bothered with it or was just too busy with other "more important" things. But, in the end, the sons were wicked and God was displeased. God judged Eli, predicting the deaths of Eli's sons, and all three men—Eli and his two sons—died, Eli's sons in battle and Eli when he heard of their deaths (1 Samuel 2:12-36 and 4:12-18).

With this dismal tale ringing in our ears, let's look to God's Word for His plan for you to honor, respect, obey, and love your parents. As you read these scriptures, ask God to show you how you can do a better job in the submission department. Pinpoint areas that need immediate first aid.

> *Children, obey your parents in the Lord, for this is right. "Honor your father and mother"—which is the first commandment with a promise—"that it may go well with you and that you may enjoy long life on the earth"* (Ephesians 6:1-3).

> *Children, obey your parents in everything, for this pleases the Lord* (Colossians 3:20).

Yes, But How?

Okay. We now know that God's Word says to obey your parents and to honor them. Now the question is, exactly *how* can you follow through on God's Word as a young woman after God's own heart who does all God's will? How can you head down God's path of obedience in this vital area? Here are a few pointers. And I think that as you read them you'll find that a heart that submits boils down to paying attention to the little things...which add up to a big thing. What are some of these little things?

1. *Your attitude*—Here's a *big* little thing! Your attitude has to do with your moods. And your moods can be right and godly, or they can be sinful. Stop for a minute and think about your attitude. Is it generally cheerful, helpful, energetic, agreeable, positive, giving, respectful? Or do you tend to mope around, grunt and grumble, resent your parents, your family, your responsibilities, even your life as a teenager? Is your day (and your life) filled with anger? Do you seem to be stomping through your days, rolling over anyone and everyone who gets in your path? (Hmmm, is this sounding like the two opposite behaviors seen in Mary and Martha from chapter 1?)

   You and I both know where our attitude is born, cultivated, and maintained, don't we? It's in our quiet time, as God's Word fills our empty hearts and sets the direction for our day...and as we pray! God's Word points the way, and prayer to God joins our hearts in agreement with God's way. And we need a huge attitude adjustment each and every day. If we fail to have this all-important time with God, we are doomed for the day. And so is everyone else! They better beware, give us a wide path, and stay out of our way!

Now, think again...what is the title of our book? Right, it's *A Young Woman After God's Own Heart*. And such a woman seeks to walk with God and to walk in all His ways and to show forth the graciousness of Christ. So, purpose along with me to...

- seek the Lord's help daily through His Word and prayer

- seek an "I'm #3" attitude (with your father as #1 and your mother as #2)

- seek to put away self-*ish*ness and put on self-*less*ness.

2. *Your room*—We'll spend more time on this topic later, but for now think about your place, your room, your space. Wherever it is and whoever you share it with (you know, your sister!), realize that your room is a part of your parents' home. Sure, you're responsible for it, but it's not yours—it's theirs. It belongs to your parents. And realizing that should make a difference. You honor your parents as you honor their property.

So I want to encourage you to have an "extra mile" attitude (there's that word again!) when it comes to your room. Whatever your parents are asking of you in terms of neatness, cleanliness, noise, rules, guests, etc., go the extra mile and do it even better and with a cheerful spirit. It's just like Jesus said, "If someone forces you to go one mile, go with him two miles" (Matthew 5:41).

I want you to take a break now—a pause. You've done a great job of hanging in there on a difficult but vital topic. Congratulations! I'm very proud of you in the Lord.

Submission certainly is a difficult area for everyone. What makes it difficult is that many times we think we know more or know better than the person we are to submit to. It's like this: I have no problem submitting to someone who is asking me to do something in an area where I know absolutely nothing, something like flying an airplane or going through a medical exam or procedure. But boy-oh-boy! do I have a hard time submitting in an area or to a person when I *think* I have some knowledge or understanding. That's where the struggle begins.

But, dear one, God calls us to be women after His own heart. And His high calling requires a heart that submits. Now…how are you doing so far?

Things to Do Today to Develop a Heart That Submits

♡ Before we go on, read again the definition of what it means to honor your parents. Then think of one thing you can do today to honor your father and mother. Follow through at your first opportunity. And don't forget to do the same tomorrow…and tomorrow…and tomorrow and….

♡ Do an attitude check. How would you describe your general attitude around the house? (How do you think your parents would describe it? Your brothers and sisters?) Then do an attitude adjustment. What specific changes will you (not *could* you or *should* you, but *will* you) make? Don't forget to ask God for His grace in this matter!

♡ Quick…is there something, anything! you can do right this minute to take care of your room? Anything you've been neglecting, putting off, or just plain ol' rebelling against doing? Honor your parents by doing it now.

Would You Like to Know More?
Check It Out

✓ Read 1 Peter 5:5-6. Here God describes the beauty of a heart of humility. Make two lists. In the first list note what your role is, and in the second note what God's role is. We know God never fails. Are you failing to obey in any way? What changes will you make?

✓ Read Luke 2:41-52. Jot down the details of this family scene—the people and places mentioned and what happened. In the end, what was Jesus' response to His parents? What do you learn from Jesus' example about submission to parents?

✓ What do these scriptures teach us about Jesus' submission to His Father's will?

Matthew 26:39   Matthew 26:42

John 4:34   John 6:38

John 15:10   Hebrews 10:7

Again, what do you learn from Jesus' example?

7

A Heart That Submits

PART 2

Honor Christ by
submitting to each other.
EPHESIANS 5:21 (TLB)

How's your heart coming along, my dear traveling companion?

Do you remember our "Heart Response" section in chapter 5? We discovered that developing a heart that obeys—that obeys God's Word—was the step on the path to becoming a woman after God's own heart that would be most meaningful on our journey. And it is soooo true! Obedience to what God says in His Word is what prepares us to respond now in this important area of submitting to parents.

And I pray that you are beginning to see the importance of submitting to your parents. Did you think *submission* was a passing phase in your life? Did you think, "If I can just grin and bear it, if I can just submit when it's convenient, then someday this 'submission thing' will be over and I'll be free to do anything and everything and act as I please"?

If you still feel this way, please forgive me. Perhaps I have failed to properly communicate the importance of submission as a lifelong process and as a lifestyle for all of God's children. Submission is the training ground for everything that is future in your (and my) life. And, as it's been said, "a child has to learn obedience in the home or he will never learn obedience to the Heavenly Father."[13]

Let's continue on now where we left off in our last chapter. Let's look at a few more of the little things you can do to train yourself in the heart and art of submission. So far we've considered *your attitude* and *your room*. Let's pick up at the "Yes, But How?" section.

3. *Your cooperation*—Have you ever been in a play? Or danced in a ballet? Or been on a sports team? As you well know, everyone had to cooperate to make the show or the game the best it could be. You all had to be a team, right?

    Well, it's the same way in a family. There are some things God wants of His families—to live together in unity (Psalm 133:1) and to glorify Him (1 Corinthians 10:31). Your parents probably want the same things for your family and are probably trying to move your family in that direction. And your job is to cooperate. True, it may at times seem strict, and it may at times be difficult, but you need to move along with them.

    So here's how it goes. If your parents want you or your family to go to church, you go. If they want to go back to church at night, you go. If they want to go to church on Wednesday night, you go. If they want to go to family camp (and it just happens to be the same weekend something great is happening at school), you go. If they need you to watch your little brother or sister while they run errands, you do it. If they need help around the house, you give it. If they are saving up for something special and have to cut the budget, you gladly give up a few trinkets or clothes or outings with your friends. In other words, you cooperate.

4. *Your help*—This may seem like a repeat of what's above, but it may just be my only chance to say this: Every person on the face of the earth yearns to hear these four little words—"How can I help?" So I encourage you at home and with your parents and family members to constantly be asking, "How can I help?" (And don't be afraid of what they may answer. For one thing, they'll probably fall off their chairs in disbelief!) As the Bible says, two are always better than one (Ecclesiastes 4:9). So offer your help.

5. *Your prayers*—Let's rewind for a second. Do you remember several chapters back when we talked about the importance of prayer? We agreed that prayer is important, that prayer changes things, and that prayer changes us. And that change includes our hearts. Well, it's pretty obvious, isn't it, that we must, must, *must* pray for our parents. Here's how it works: If your parents have an annoying habit or way of

dealing with things, pray for them. If they don't get along with each other, pray for them. If they pick on your little brother, pray for them. If they are stressed out, pray for them. You can never pray too much for your parents!

And keep on praying for yourself, too. If you think you don't even like your parents, pray for yourself. If you think they're stupid or dumb or out of it, pray for yourself. If you think what they're asking of you is unfair, pray for yourself. If you think your parents are too strict, pray for yourself. If you think they don't understand you, pray for yourself.

And what are you asking of God? Ask Him to soften your heart, to change your attitude (there's that word again!), to give you the special help of His grace, to give you a greater appreciation for your parents, to help you to submit, honor, and respect them. Ask God to work not only in your parents' hearts, but also in yours! That's what a woman after God's own heart does.

6. *Your submission*—As a Christian, you'll be hearing the word "submission" a lot! The Bible calls us to submit to about everyone you can think of—the government, bosses (1 Peter 2:13-18), the church (Hebrews 13:17), even to one another (Ephesians 5:21). But your home and your relationships there are the training ground for your submission to all others, including your future submission to a hus-

band (Ephesians 5:22). Therefore, you honor your parents and submit yourself to them.

Submission is a challenge straight from God to you. It's a measure of your spiritual maturity. Why? Because no one can make you submit to anyone else. You must choose to do it yourself. Your parents can't make you, your friends can't make you, and your youth leader can't make you. No, you have to decide to submit *yourself* to your parents. And here's the shocker—if you aren't submitting to your parents now, you aren't submitting to God, and you'll probably have trouble fulfilling God's desire for you to submit to your future husband's leadership. That's pretty far-reaching, isn't it?

7. *Your truthfulness*—Everyone wants to enjoy good communication with others. Well, good communication at home begins with your being truthful to your parents. An author I know and respect shared this story from her teenage days. Her friend received a new car for her sixteenth birthday and stopped by to take her for a ride. But somewhere during the course of their ride, another girl, who didn't have a driver's license, took the wheel and began driving. And, wouldn't you know it—there was a car wreck! At this point her "friends" asked her to lie about who was driving. Well, as the parents began to arrive on the scene of the wreck, the first words out of the mothers' mouths were, "Who was driving the car?" After my friend chose to tell the truth (and go against

the wishes of her cohorts), one mother said, "I've already talked to a neighbor who saw the three of you go by, and she told me who was driving. If you had lied to me, I wouldn't have trusted you again."[14]

Things get sticky in life. And sometimes we end up in situations we didn't choose, like this teenager did. But no matter what happens to you, you must always tell the truth. That's what a woman after God's own heart does. Why? Because, first of all, she shouldn't have anything to hide if she's walking on God's path of obedience. And second, truthfulness is the foundation of all good relationships...especially your relationship with your parents. So make it your habit to tell the truth. It's a habit of noble character.

8. *Your giving*—If I could wish one thing for you, if I could have one prayer answered for you as you read and complete this book, it would be this: I would pray that you begin today to go through life as a giver. You see, the world seems to be divided into two kinds of people—those who give and those who take. One, the giver, is *other*-oriented and the other, the taker, is *self*-oriented. Those who think of others are Christlike, and those who think only of themselves tend to lie and cheat, manipulate and connive. Their hearts are set on themselves and not on Christ or on others.

So, my dear friend, I want you to be a giver! I want you to make a difference in the lives of other people.

I want you to join with me in my goal to better the life of every person God allows to cross my path. I want you to be constantly asking the Lord and your heart, "What can I give?" in every situation. And "every situation" includes first and foremost your situation at home. Why? Because *what you are at home is what you are.*

Here's a little visual aid. Imagine that you are the richest person in the world. It's in your power to bless everyone else in the whole world because you have so much to give and share with others. Then imagine yourself walking down a path or a road or a street (or a corridor at school). And there you are...literally throwing your riches away, exuberantly tossing them to everyone you meet. You smile! You greet them! And you give them something!

Oh, how I want this woman to be you! (And oh, how I want this woman to be me!) And if you think about it, we do have everything to give! We have life in Christ (2 Timothy 1:1). We have been blessed by God with all spiritual blessings in heavenly places in Christ (Ephesians 1:3). We even have God's love, joy, peace, patience, kindness, goodness, faithfulness, gentleness, and self-control (Galatians 5:22-23). We have soooo much to give! So let's start where it counts the most—right at home—and give to those at home first. Believe me, if you can do this at home, you can do it anywhere! (Oh yes, and while you are giving, remember this principle: *Give...expecting nothing in return!* (Luke 6:35).

Heart Response

You are so wonderful for staying with me through these important heart exercises! My heart is so full of the many wonderful things I want to share with you. I don't want you to struggle and fail, to suffer and flop around like I did when I was trying to grow into a woman after God's own heart. I want you to *know* what God's great plan is for your life as His woman. I guess I'm trying to give you some shortcuts to spiritual growth. My vision for you is large. It's grand! There is so much God desires for you. And I desire it, too!

Now, please, don't leave this chapter without making your own heart response to God's Word regarding a heart that submits. Check your heart. How's your attitude? What's going on in your room? Are you cooperating with your parents? Are you lending your help as well as your prayers? Is yours a heart of submission, of truthfulness, and of a sweet giving spirit? Pray along with David,

> *Search me, O God, and know my heart;*
> *test me and know my anxious thoughts.*
> *See if there is any offensive way in me,*
> *and lead me in the way everlasting.*

Psalm 139:23-24

Things to Do Today to Develop a Heart That Submits

♡ Practice saying "How can I help?" three times in front of your mirror. Then go to your mother and say it to her. (P.S., be prepared to catch her when she faints!)

♡ Think about your cooperation and your submission in your family. What are the three things you find most difficult to do in these areas of family unity? Put these three things on your daily prayer list for yourself...then pray to cooperate and submit the next time they come up.

♡ Determine—just for today—to be more giving to your family members. Determine to give away your smile, your warm greeting, your loving touch, your helping hand, and your kind words of encouragement. Do it...no matter what the response. Do as Jesus did—"He went around doing good" (Acts 10:38).

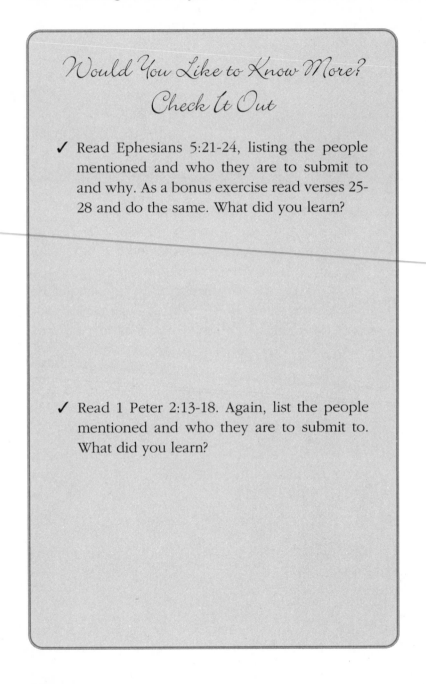

Would You Like to Know More?
Check It Out

✓ Read Ephesians 5:21-24, listing the people mentioned and who they are to submit to and why. As a bonus exercise read verses 25-28 and do the same. What did you learn?

✓ Read 1 Peter 2:13-18. Again, list the people mentioned and who they are to submit to. What did you learn?

✓ Continue looking at God's plan for the family by reading Ephesians 6:1-4 and Colossians 3:18-21. List the instructions given to each family member. Did you find yourself here? And are you demonstrating a heart devoted to God by obeying God's instructions to you, or do you need to make some changes? What changes?

✓ Now prayerfully read 1 Peter 2:21-24. Write out how Jesus submitted to His Father's will for His life. Then write out a prayer of thanksgiving to God for sending His Son to die for sin—*your* sin—and for Jesus' obedience to His Father's will.

8

A Heart That Loves

A new command I give you:
Love one another...By this all men
will know that you are my disciples,
if you love one another.

JOHN 13:34-35

If you're like me, you admire the men and women of the Bible who exhibited great faith and hearts after God. Well, may I introduce you to three giants of the faith? Each of them loved God. Each of them obeyed God. And each of them served God to their last dying breath.

The first is probably the most well known. His name is Moses. Wow, what a man of God! In fact, he's been dubbed "the greatest Jewish leader."[15] Moses not only led the Israelites out of Egypt, but he was also the man who received the Ten Commandments from God. Moses had a pretty rough life, but he was devoted to God and ultimately became a prophet for God and the writer of the first five books of the Bible, called the Pentateuch. We can definitely say that Moses was "sold out" to God.

The second giant is Aaron. This godly man was the first high priest of God in Israel. Talk about a privilege! He was also the man God chose to communicate to the king of Egypt for Moses, to be Moses' right-hand man, and to speak for Moses. Aaron, too, was certainly sold out for God.

The third giant is actually a giant-*ess*, a woman. Her name is Miriam. This woman was a prophetess, a leader of women, a woman who wrote songs of praise to God and knew how to use her head under pressure. Miriam, too, was sold out for God.

Now, here's something else about this awesome three-some—they were siblings! They were two brothers and a sister that God used mightily. They were family.

Love Your Brothers and Sisters

It's sad to hear someone say that her brother or sister is her biggest headache in life. To quote the apostle James, "Surely, this is not right!" (James 3:10 TLB).

And it's not! God wants His families to love one another and to serve Him. And the Bible contains a good number of brothers and sisters who served God together as a team. For instance,

- Siblings Aaron and Moses and Miriam served God together.

- Brothers Peter and Andrew followed Jesus and became two of His twelve disciples (Matthew 4:18 and 10:2).

- Brothers James and John followed Jesus and became two of His twelve disciples (Matthew 4:21). In fact, Jesus nicknamed these two brothers "Sons of Thunder" (Mark 3:17).

- Sisters Mary and Martha and their brother, Lazarus, were devoted followers of Jesus. Together they faithfully cared for Jesus and His disciples (Luke 10:38; John 12:1-2).

Where, we wonder, is such dynamic teamwork born? Well, my friend, it's born in a home. It's born in a family. And it's born out of love—love for God and love for one another.

✎ *From God's Word to Your Heart...*

What is the secret to healthy relationships between brothers and sisters? In a word, it's love. Hear what our Savior and the apostle Paul had to say about love. As you read along, think about what these verses teach us about love. And think even more specifically about what they teach us about loving our brothers and sisters. Do you need to make any changes in your attitude toward your siblings, in your treatment of them?

> *A new command I give you: Love one another.... By this all men will know that you are my disciples, if you love one another* (John 13:34-35).

> *If anyone says, "I love God," yet hates his brother, he is a liar. For anyone who does not love his brother, whom he has seen, cannot love God, whom he has not seen. And he has given us this command: Whoever loves God must also love his brother* (1 John 4:20-21).

> *When the Holy Spirit controls our lives, he will produce this kind of fruit in us: love...patience, kindness, goodness...gentleness and self control* (Galatians 5:22-23 NLT).

Yes, But How?

There are many ways we show concern and demonstrate a heart of love when it comes to our family members. We discussed some of those ways in the previous chapter in the area of our relationship with our parents. But now let's turn our eyes (and hearts!) toward our brothers and sisters, whether older or younger. I'll share several important areas that speak loudly of love. Maybe you will think of others along the way. If you do, jot them down at the end of the chapter. Whatever you do, seek to develop a heart that loves, especially a heart that loves those in your family circle.

1. *Respect one another*—When you show respect for the territory, room, possessions, and privacy of another person, your relationship with that person will improve tremendously. And right away! You know how you feel when your privacy is violated, when others help themselves to your things without asking, when someone barges into your room without knocking or asking, when someone reads your personal journal or diary or mail...or email! Well, you need to respect the space of others exactly like you want your space respected. Even if you share your room with your sister, a part of that room is *her* territory. So why not begin improving your relationships with your family members by showing a greater respect for them by respecting what is theirs?

2. *Listen to one another*—In any friendship, communication is nine-tenths of the relationship. You know how it is with a best friend—you could talk to them for hours...which means you are listening for part of that time! So make it your goal to learn better communication skills inside your family. If you can talk to one another, you can become friends—even best friends! And listening is a large part of connecting with one another. So get creative. Reach out. Set up a regular Coke date with your brother or sister. When a sibling is swimming in the pool, join him or her and maybe just float along on a raft, talking, sharing, asking questions, catching up. If you share your room with a sister or two, get an update on

their lives after lights-out at night. And, by all means, pray with your brothers and sisters...and for them. It doesn't have to be anything long or heavy, just the heartfelt prayer of a loving sister. Don't worry if they think it's dumb or stupid. They'll get used to it and grow to appreciate it. And then don't be surprised if they start coming to you with their problems and asking you to please pray with them!

3. *Serve one another*—God has given us ears to hear and eyes to see (Proverbs 20:12). And it's hard to live under the same roof and not see and hear how your brothers and sisters could use a little assistance from someone...anyone!...even *you!* So ask God to make you more sensitive to the needs of your siblings, to serving them. Ask Him to open your ears and eyes (and heart!). For instance, when you see your sister or brother carrying a heavy load or backpack up the steps to the front door, jump up and say, "Let me get that door for you." Also, we all lose things (and you know how frustrating that can be!). So volunteer to help out in the search. And when you're doing your laundry and find your brother's or sister's laundry in the dryer, take it to them and say "Here's your laundry out of the dryer. Do you want me to help you fold it?"

4. *Help one another*—We covered this same point in our chapter regarding your parents, so hopefully this Christlike attitude is becoming ingrained in your

daily behavior. But do the same for your siblings. Ask them, too, "How can I help?" When they're stewing over their homework, late getting out the door, trying to learn their Bible verses for their Bible club meeting, lend a helping hand and an understanding heart. Be on the lookout for ways to help out. Everyone appreciates—and needs(!)—a helping hand.

5. *Share with one another*—When I say share with one another, I don't mean just clothes and things. I mean to also share ideas and dreams. If you can unlock another's heart, then you can be a better pray-er, encourager, supporter, and helper to that person...even if that person just happens to be your brother or sister! And while you're at it, don't forget to share the truths and the verses you are learning from the Bible. And share in worship together. You never know when one of these shared experiences will mark your sibling's life. You never know when the verse you passed on verbally or in a written note will be just what they needed to get through a rough day! The more you can share together, the better friends you become.

6. *Touch one another*—I have two things I want to say in this area of touching one another. The first is positive and the second is negative. So, first the positive. I love it when I see brothers and sisters walking arm in arm or with their arms around each other,

hugging, patting each other on the back, even giving high fives. Such affection is a privilege and an out-working of the natural closeness that comes with being a part of a family. In many ways, no one else has that privilege. So be generous with your hugs and genuine affection.

But then there is the negative. One day when my husband and I were checking into a hotel, a family was waiting behind us in the check-in line. During the entire time we were dealing with the hotel clerk, the three kids in the family (who were all in their teens) were kicking each other's bottoms, slugging each other in the arms, slapping at each other's faces, and doing a few other physical things to each other I won't even mention(!)...while the parents did nothing. It was clear that in this family physical "affection" and touching had gone way too far! I felt sorry (and angry) for the daughter/sister whose body and dignity were treated with such disrespect by her brothers. And I felt sorry (and angry) that the two cute teenage boys were allowed to treat their sister, a young woman, in such a disrespectful way. To think that these crude brothers were the future boyfriends and husbands of some other poor girls out there made me sick.

So I'm saying to you, regardless of where (or how low!) your "family standard" has fallen, of where your parents have or have not drawn the lines and set the boundaries, *you* must treat the bodies and persons of your brothers and sisters with utmost respect and dignity. *No inappropriate touching!* I'm sure you would want the same thing for yourself. So begin with yourself and "do to others as you would have them to do to you" (Luke 6:31).

7. *Pray for one another*—Here it is again! Prayer! You simply cannot pray for your brothers and sisters enough! And remember, too, that when you pray for others, God changes your heart, gives you His love and wisdom, and many times moves in the hearts of those you pray for. So think of the grandest thing you could ask of God for your siblings. Do they need to know Christ? Then pray! Do they need to get along better with Mom and Dad? Then pray! Do they need a friend, a job, better grades? Then pray! Are they trying to make an important decision, like whether or not to go to college, or which college? Then pray! Is one of them in a doubtful relationship with a boyfriend or girlfriend? Then pray! The Bible commands us to "pray for each other" (James 5:16) and assures us that God's ears are open to our prayers (1 Peter 3:12). So take the time to pray for your brothers and sisters. As someone known as "the kneeling Christian" once said, "Prayer is our highest privilege, our gravest responsibility, and the greatest power God has put into our hands." Who knows what God may do?!

8. *Encourage one another*—Everyone can use encouragement. All teens struggle with schoolwork and

grades, as well as with making friends and getting along. Yes, everyone can use a friendly word of encouragement from a sister who comes alongside them with cheerfulness. Everyone can use a "Way to go! Good job! Hang in there! You're the best! I'm so glad I'm your sister." And don't forget to encourage one another in the Lord. That's what two famous friends in the Bible did. Jonathan and David encouraged one another to "find strength in God" (1 Samuel 23:16).

As I said earlier, everyone yearns for a close relationship with someone who respects, helps, shares, encourages, and listens to them. And that includes your brothers and sisters! So why not be that someone in their lives? Why not put on a heart that loves and make loving those under your own roof your first priority in the love department?

Heart Response

We began this all-important chapter by looking at a team of two brothers and a sister who were mightily used by God. How refreshing! And how inspiring!

Unfortunately, however, the Bible also contains stories of siblings who are anything but what God desires. For instance, Cain killed his brother Abel (Genesis 4:8). Sisters Rachel and Leah hated and envied one another (Genesis

30:1). And Joseph's brothers hated and envied him so much that they sold him to slave traders (Genesis 37:26-27).

So I want to end our time discussing family matters with the greatest "how" of all when it comes to a heart that loves. It is God's commandment to us to *love one another.* Here's a definition of love that opened my eyes to what it means to love one another: *Love* is a feeling of the mind as much as of the heart; it concerns the will as much as the emotions; it describes the deliberate effort that we can make only with the help of God.

In short, love is not an emotion, but an action. Love is the things we do...and hold back from doing. And love is a decision. Love is an act of the will. Plus, praise God, we have His help in showing forth His fruit of the Spirit, His love, in our hearts and our lives when we look to Him (Galatians 5:22)!

So...let's push family quarrels aside and let the love of God reside in our hearts. Let's become *sisters* after God's own heart!

Things to Do Today to Develop
a Heart That Loves

♡ Write a little note of encouragement to each brother or sister.

♡ Be on the lookout for ways to serve your siblings. Volunteer to help, too.

♡ Set up a page in your prayer notebook for each of your brothers and sisters. (And don't forget to pray!)

Would You Like to Know More?
Check It Out

✓ The story of Miriam's love for her baby brother, Moses, can be found in Exodus 2:1-10. How does Miriam's helpfulness to her mother and her concern for her baby brother touch your heart?

✓ The story of Miriam, Aaron, and Moses' joint service to God is highlighted in Exodus 15:1,20-21 as they celebrate God's deliverance of His people. How does the example of this threesome challenge you in your relationship with your siblings?

✓ Sadly, the story of Miriam and Aaron's jealousy against their brother, Moses, darkens an otherwise good relationship (Numbers 12:1-16). How does their envy of their brother speak to your heart?

✓ God's Word defines "love" in 1 Corinthians 13:4-7. What areas do you need to work on in your relationships with your brothers and sisters?

9

A Heart That Cares

The wise woman builds her house.

PROVERBS 14:1

Having two daughters has provided me with one particular glad/sad occasion many times. That repeated occasion was the day each fall when I drove my girls and all their belongings to their college campus and helped them move into their dormitory rooms for another year of schooling. Of course I was glad that they were growing up, glad that they were taking on the challenge of attempting a college education, and glad for the many wonderful friends and adventures that awaited them. But there's no getting around it—it made me sad to say good-bye to my daughters, who were also my friends. And it especially made me sad to deposit them into a stark, bare, empty dorm room containing absolutely nothing but an exposed mattress. More than once, I cried my way home!

But soon that much-anticipated evening came—Parents Night—when Jim and I (along with all the other parents of collegians) were invited to tour the dormitories. Well, I just cannot describe to you the joy and surprise we received when we entered our daughters' cubicles! Their rooms had been miraculously transformed! What had once been forlorn was filled with the beautiful and the unique as Katherine and Courtney sought to express themselves in their individual rooms. There were ruffles and frills, dried flowers and ribbons, pictures and posters, tea sets and fish bowls, candles and baskets with live ivy plants. Music was playing and special lighting and lamps created a warm glow.

I'm sure I don't have to tell you that I left Parents Night with a much happier heart! Why? Because my girls now had a home away from home. But more amazing than what I saw was knowing that each of my daughters had done it herself. Each had taken her own "things" from her real home and used them to create a second home. In the end, they had turned nothing—barren look-alike dorm rooms—into something, beautiful expressions of their beautiful hearts.

Your Own Home-Sweet-Home

Just how did my daughters' abilities blossom? And just where did they learn to decorate, to "fuss," to express themselves, to feather a nest, to clean and organize, to make beautiful crafts, to create places that ministered not only to them but to the countless others who passed through their doorways in the college dorm?

Well, the answer is summed up in a single word—they learned these homemaking skills at *home*. And their learning experience was a co-partnership between my daughters and me. Here's how it happened.

I've said before that I did not grow up as a Christian. Therefore I started out as a baby Christian at age 28…and at ground zero in the homemaking department! I was a remedial learner, one that was definitely behind and desperately needed help. But I was also an eager learner. Boy oh boy, did I ever have a need to know! I had been married eight years and had two tiny preschoolers and a pigpen for a home!

But as I began to read my brand-new Bible, I took a pink highlighter in hand and began to mark everything I read that had to do with being a Christian woman, wife, mother, and homemaker. As God spoke to my heart through His Word, my knowledge of who God wanted me to be and what God wanted me to do grew. And it wasn't long before my eager heart responded. It was then that I learned to build my own home-sweet-home so that my family could be blessed. I bought and read books, I met with older and wiser women, and I worked hard. But I finally "got it"!

Not wanting my Katherine and Courtney to suffer in ignorance (and sloppiness) as I had, I began teaching them what I was learning. Then, whatever I was doing to take care of my "house" (the entire house), my girls were doing in their "little house" (their room), in their own home-sweet-home.

✎ *From God's Word to Your Heart…*

Exactly what do you and I find in the Bible that tells us what God has in mind for us as women after His own heart in the area of our home-sweet-home? Here are a few key scriptures. As you read them, please think of things you might need to do to improve. Do you need an attitude change? Do you need better skills? Do you need help?

The wise woman builds her house, but with her own hands the foolish one tears hers down (Proverbs 14:1).

By wisdom a house is built...through knowledge its rooms are filled with rare and beautiful treasures (Proverbs 24:3-4).

[A woman of noble character] watches over the affairs of her household and does not eat the bread of idleness (Proverbs 31:27).

The older women [are to]...train the younger women...to be busy [workers] at home (Titus 2:3-5).

Yes, But How?

These verses paint a picture of what a woman of wisdom does—she builds and takes care of and watches over and works away at creating a home-sweet-home. As an unmarried woman, that home is wherever you happen to live. Whether you live in your own room in your parents' house or share it with a sister or two (I know of one family whose four girls share the same room!), whether you live in an apartment or a dorm room like my daughters did, the place where you live is yours to "build." It's yours to turn into your own home-sweet-home.

So here are a few how-to's on home-sweet-home building.

1. *Learn the basics*—There are only a handful of simple basics involved in taking care of your room. They are dusting, vacuuming, cleaning, doing laundry, and organizing. And like any skill, these are learned by repetition. The more you do anything, the easier it becomes...until soon you can almost do it without thinking.

   I taught my daughters these basics, and together the three of us did them over and over and over until we were all able to do them quickly. Then, miracle of miracles(!), a certain amount of joy set in as we admired our handiwork. Our faces shone (like our clean rooms) with a sense of pride in the end result and the rewarding feeling of accomplishment.

But here's the greatest blessing. When Katherine and Courtney got married, guess what? Homemaking was no big deal! Taking care of a "home" was no problem! Why? Because they had basically been doing it all their lives in their own little home-sweet-home, in their room. Their knowledge of the basics left them with only one new major assignment as newlyweds—learning how to be *wives!* And then along came the babies and another new major assignment—learning how to be *mothers!* (I'm sure you get the picture!)

2. *Do your share*—Wherever you live and whoever you share it with, whether family or roommates, be sure you do your part of the work. Don't try to get out of work. That's a bad habit to develop and a hard one to break! Instead make it a goal to do your part and to do it excellently! As the Bible says, "Whatever your hand finds to do, do it with all your might" and "Whatever you do, work at it with all your heart, as working for the Lord, not for men" (Ecclesiastes 9:10 and Colossians 3:23). This is also a good place to put Jesus' "extra mile" concept to work in your heart (Matthew 5:41) by doing *more than* your share!

3. *Volunteer to help*—If your mom's in the kitchen preparing a meal, volunteer to help her. You'll be amazed at what you'll learn. (I just heard a mother of six say that all her children learned to cook at age seven, that every one of her children could fix his

or her own food if it were necessary. She explained that they rotate nights cooking with her in the kitchen, but each fixes his or her favorite dishes. Now, that's motivating!) So volunteer! And don't forget how much everyone loves to hear those words, "How can I help?" Make it a point to be like Jesus, "who went around doing good" (Acts 10:38). Remember His words, how He said "It is more blessed to give than to receive" (Acts 20:35). And remember, too, that He told us to give "without expecting to get anything back" (Luke 6:35).

4. *Get help if you need it*—Like the instruction in Titus 2:3-5 said, women are to teach one another how to take care of their homes. So, if you need help, go get it. Ask for it. Whether that assistance comes from your mom or from someone else, seek help in this vital area of being a woman after God's own heart.

5. *Develop a heart that cares*—Did you notice the title of this chapter? I titled it "A Heart That Cares." And that's the key for both you and me when it comes to our place at home. We simply must care. And it helps me to care when I know that *God* wants me to care. And it helps me to care when I acknowledge that *what I am at home is what I am.* I'm either messy or I'm neat. I'm either buried under things or I'm on top of things. I'm either unorganized or I'm orderly. I'm either living in chaos or I have a plan that I'm following. I'm either a flake or I'm dependable.

So ask yourself (as I ask myself often), How am I doing when it comes to my place, my finances, my clothes? What character qualities are being evidenced by my care for my place? Your answers will tell the whole tale (and I'm hoping it's a good one!).

6. *Set aside time*—The biggest challenge to taking care of your home-sweet-home is always finding the *time!* So you must *make* the time. How? Each week take your calendar in hand and mark off an hour or two for taking care of your room. That's about how long it will take to run your laundry through the washer and dryer, to dust and vacuum your room, and arrange the contents of your drawers. Yes, you may have a little cleaning to do in your bathroom and on some trouble spots on your desktop and mirrors, but that will only take minutes. Then stick to your plan. If a friend calls, set another time to get together or have her come over *after* you've cleaned your room! What a nice reward for you…and what a nice treat for your friend (not to mention your family!). Which reminds me, don't forget that the place where you live—your room—really isn't yours. It belongs to your parents! So be sure to work at this next how-to.

7. *Follow these "Golden Rules for Living"*—They will not only help you build your own home-sweet-home, but they will help you get along with those you must share it with!

If you open it, close it.

If you turn it on, turn it off.

If you unlock it, lock it up.

If you break it, admit it.

If you can't fix it, call in someone who can.

If you borrow it, return it.

If you value it, take care of it.

If you make a mess, clean it up.

If you move it, put it back.

If it belongs to someone else, get permission to use it.

If you don't know how to operate it, leave it alone.

If it's none of your business, don't ask questions.[16]

Heart Response

Dear sister and friend, are you catching God's vision for you and your place? Do you see the value of learning to care about the place where you live? Of learning to do what it takes to take care of the place where you live?

Take an inventory of your own heart attitude toward that precious place you call home, the place where you live, your place. If you couldn't care less about the looks of your special place, ask God to perform open-heart surgery in you. Ask Him to open it up and give you a heart that cares.

We've talked about how your homelife is the training ground for your future relationship with a husband and children of your own (if the Lord wills). Well, dear one, home is also the training ground for your work ethic, whether that work ethic is used in the home as a homemaker, on a job, or on the mission field. If and when you get married, get a job, or serve on the mission field, you take yourself and the character qualities you've learned at home (by taking care of yourself and your room) with you. You will either be sloppy in your place of service, or you'll be meticulous. You will either be lazy and unreliable, or you'll be diligent. You will either be unimaginative, or you'll be creative. You will either be disorderly, or you'll be organized. You will either be haphazard and sporadic, or you'll operate on a plan and a schedule. You see, you will take what you *are* with you! *What you are at home is what you are!*

So what is it that will make the difference? The answer is found in the attitude you are developing right now at home. The care you take with yourself, of your own things and the things of others at home, and the effort you make at home today will extend into your future. *What you will be tomorrow, you are becoming today.*

Things to Do Today to Develop a Heart That Cares

♡ Make a list of all the "touches" and tasks that are needed to make your room a home-sweet-home.

♡ Are there any basics that you need help on? If so, who will you ask for help?

♡ Mark off some time on your schedule this week to begin working your way through your list.

Would You Like to Know More?
Check It Out

✓ The many works of love done by the woman honored in Proverbs 31 prove her love for her home and her family. Read Proverbs 31:10-31. What strikes you most? And which of her efforts can you put into practice to better your life and the place that is your home-sweet-home?

✓ Regarding the Proverbs 31 woman, what character qualities are evident in God's description of her? Once again, what strikes you most? And which of her sterling qualities can you (or *must* you) seek to develop in your life and heart?

10

A Heart That Chooses Wisely

He who walks with the wise grows wise,
but a companion of fools suffers harm.

PROVERBS 13:20

This past week I heard my sweet, kind, patient, understanding husband, Jim, on the phone with our cell phone service. It seems that I had gone over the number of minutes that we pay for every month on my cell phone account. I was horrified...because we already pay for quite a few minutes! But more? I knew that most of those minutes were spent talking to lots of people about lots of things that had nothing to do with friends and friendships. Yet I also knew some of those many minutes (how many, I wondered?) had also been spent talking to my friends.

My friends are important to me as I'm sure yours are to you. And, my dear friend, that's as it should be. You see, the Bible says you and I are created in the image of God

(Genesis 1:26). That means we resemble God in some very special ways. And one of those ways is that, like God, we are social beings. That means...

- *We have fellowship with God*—God created us to have fellowship with Himself. God doesn't *need* us as friends, but He *chooses* to be our friend and to fellowship with us, and

- *We have friendship with Jesus Christ*—God's Son, Jesus, has chosen us to be His friends. Jesus said, "You are my friends....I have called you friends" (John 15:14-15).

Understanding this very special relationship we enjoy with God and the friendship we have with Jesus points to yet another priority area for a woman after God's own heart—*she chooses her earthly friendships wisely.* Not only is her spiritual relationship with God important, but her physical, human relationships are also important.

The Bible gives us a perfect example of a healthy, biblical friendship in the lives of David and Jonathan. We'll look at their remarkable friendship later, but for now, understand that Jonathan was an extremely committed friend to David, and vice versa. In fact, Jonathan hung in there with David, actually helping David to escape the repeated attempts of murder by Jonathan's own father! David and Jonathan can teach you and me a lot about what it means to choose our friends wisely.

Finding a Friend

But how can you and I find a friend like a David or a Jonathan? Of course, the best first step (always and in all things) is to see what God says about friends in His Word, the Bible. Let's see what He has to say about friends and about how to choose wisely.

✎ *From God's Word to Your Heart...*

The Bible is very clear and specific when it tells us what kind of person to look for in a friend...and what kind to avoid like the plague! First let's look at God's list of people to reject as friends. As you read through these verses, make a mental note about the speech, character, and conduct of those who are most definitely *not* to be your friends. You can pray for them, and you should be friendly to them, but they are not to be your friends. What are the warning signals to beware of? (P.S., God's warnings apply to friends of the opposite sex as well!) (And another P.S.— in the Hebrew language, the language the book of Proverbs is written in, the word "friend" and "neighbor" are the same.)

> *Blessed is the person who does not walk in the counsel of the wicked or stand in the way of sinners or sit in the seat of mockers* (Psalm 1:1).

Do not set foot on the path of the wicked or walk in the way of evil men (Proverbs 4:14).

He who walks with the wise grows wise, but a companion of fools suffers harm (Proverbs 13:20).

A violent man entices his neighbor and leads him down a path that is not good (Proverbs 16:29).

Do not make friends with a hot-tempered man, do not associate with one easily angered, or you may learn his ways and get yourself ensnared (Proverbs 22:24-25).

Whoever flatters his neighbor is spreading a net for his feet (Proverbs 29:5).

But now I am writing you that you must not associate with anyone who calls himself a

*brother [a Christian] but is sexually immoral or
greedy, an idolater or a slanderer, a drunkard
or a swindler. With such a [person] do not even
eat* (1 Corinthians 5:11).

*Do not be misled: "Bad company corrupts good
character"* (1 Corinthians 15:33).

Whew! That's quite a list, isn't it? But God cares for you
and wants to protect you from those who will harm you
and influence you away from God and toward evil. So
now, how do you go about finding a friend? Take these
scriptures to heart, for they lay the groundwork for suc-
cessful friendships.

*He who walks with the wise grows wise, but a
companion of fools suffers harm* (Proverbs
13:20).

*Do not be yoked together [teamed up] with
unbelievers. For what do righteousness and
wickedness have in common? Or what fellowship can light have with darkness?... What does
a believer have in common with an unbe-
liever?* (2 Corinthians 6:14-15).

Yes, But How?

Did you notice the subtitle of this book? It's "A Teen's Guide to Friends, Faith, Family, and the Future." Well, here we are, dealing with the section about friends. Let's look at a few guidelines for finding a friend, being a friend, and building lasting and godly friendships.

1. *Follow God's rules*—God's rules will save you from a lot of heartache, mistakes, and regrets. Steer clear of people who fall on God's lists of "Do Not's" and actively seek out those who enhance your life as a Christian. And here's a hint—you'll usually find these people at church or in a Christian youth group.

   I like what one man said about friendships formed on the basis of a mutual love for God. He wrote these words to describe the qualities at the heart of the friendship between David and Jonathan: They...

   > ...assented to the same authority,

   > ...knew the same God,

   > ...were going the same way,

   > ...longed for the same things,

   > ...dreamed mutual dreams, and

   > ...yearned for the same experiences of holiness and worship.[17]

2. *Remember it's better to have no friends than to have the wrong friends*—There's nothing wrong with

being a late bloomer in the friendship department. *Hold on* to your innocence and character and *hold out* for friendships with those who make you a better Christian and a better person rather than grasping onto someone—anyone!—just to have a friend. And if you get lonely, God has provided friendships for you.

First, you have a friend in Jesus. As I said earlier, you can always turn to Jesus. Jesus said, "I have called you friends" (John 15:15). If you have a personal relationship with Jesus Christ, then, friend, you have a friend for life in Him! You are indeed His chosen friend...and His forever friend!

Second, you have friends in your parents. (Are you squirming yet? Are you wondering, "You can't be serious!"? Well, I am!) It's true! There's nothing wrong—and maybe everything right—with having your mom and dad as your best friends. It's not childish. And it's not stupid. They are God's gift to you. And believe me, no one loves you more or cares for you more deeply and genuinely than your very own mother and father.

And *third*, you have friends in your brothers and sisters. (And now are you wondering, "You must be joking now! Not my goofy brother!" No, I'm serious again!) The same thing is true of family. I can tell you from experience that your friends throughout life will come and go. You may stay in touch, talk on the phone, and email one another. But your friends will usually move on (maybe even literally moving on to another town). They will go to different colleges, get married, move away with their husbands, start their families, and...well, you get the picture. But your family will always be there, especially if you build and maintain friendships with them. As I write this, my father and my husband's parents have already died, and my mother, who suffers from Alzheimer's disease, has not known or recognized me for seven years. And guess what? We thank God every day that we still have our brothers and sisters. We delight in the anchor of these lasting family friendships.

So, dear sister, do your part. Of course you'll want to spend time with Jesus (after all, that's what we've learned that a woman after God's own heart does!). But also spend time with your parents and with your brothers and sisters. Be friends with them. Support them. Love them. You'll be building friendships that will last a lifetime.

3. *Be friendly*—I hope you've gotten the message from the Bible (and from me) about how important it is to protect yourself and to be wise when it comes to finding friends—the *right* friends. And I hope you're also understanding that you must be friendly to all, that you must be a friendly person. As a Christian woman, you have so much to give! And, as we've already learned, everyone needs a smile and a warm "hello" and a kind word, especially a word about

Jesus. You and I want to be like Jesus, who was a friend to sinners (Luke 7:34) and who "went around doing good" (Acts 10:38). So I want to end this chapter with these "Ten Commandments of Friendship."[18] Take them with you throughout your life.

- Speak to people—there is nothing as nice as a cheerful word of greeting.

- Smile at people—it takes seventy-two muscles to frown and only fourteen to smile!

- Call people by name—the sweetest music to anyone's ear is the sound of their own name.

- Be friendly and helpful—if you would have friends, be friendly.

- Be cordial—speak and act as if everything you do were a real pleasure.

- Be genuinely interested in people—you can like *everyone* if you try.

- Be generous with praise—cautious with criticism.

- Be considerate of the feelings of others—it will be appreciated.

- Be thoughtful of the opinions of others.

- Be alert to give service—what counts most in life is what we do for others!

There's no doubt that friends and friendships are important parts of your life! Friendships are part of God's plan and a major means of mutual growth, encouragement, excitement, learning, and love, not to mention witnessing and evangelism. Biblical friendships definitely bless us and build us up.

As we leave this discussion of God's guidelines for finding friends, I want to share this bit of wisdom for life with you: There seems to be three kinds of people in life—

> those who pull you down,
>
> those who pull you along, and
>
> those who pull you up.

Based on these three kinds of people, I strongly believe that your best friends should be Christians. Your best friends should be believers who pull you along and pull you up toward Christlikeness—like David and Jonathan did for one another. Your best friends should be soul partners—like David and Jonathan were. Your best friends should be strong, like-minded Christians who help you to think your best thoughts, do your noblest deeds, and be your finest self.

So as you go about the business of looking for a friend and making friends, have the highest standards possible—those we've been discussing from the Bible. First of all, have the highest standards for yourself. Don't sell yourself short. You *be* the kind of person who pulls others along and pulls them up toward the things of God.

But don't settle for anything less than God's highest standards for yourself in the "best friend" category. Those you spend your precious time and life with must love the Lord, first and foremost, in *their* hearts. And they must help *you* to love the Lord even more. *They* must possess a fiery passion for serving Jesus Christ, and they must fan the flames of *your* passion for serving Him.

Remember, when you pick your friends, you are picking your future! So choose your friends with care. You become what they are!

Things to Do Today to Develop a Heart That Chooses Wisely

♡ Review again the scriptures listed in the section titled "From God's Word to Your Heart." Summarize the teaching of each verse in a word or two. Then write out a list in your personal notebook of these guidelines regarding the kind of friend you want to be…and have. Look at it often—even every day!

♡ Make a list of your current "friends." Place these names next to your list of God's guidelines for friends. Do they all belong on your list of "best friends"? Why or why not?

♡ Make one more list—those you know who pull you along and who pull you up in your relationship with the Lord. How can you spend more time with them? (They just may be friends-in-the-making!)

Would You Like to Know More?
Check It Out

✓ Read Proverbs 1:10-19, God's instructions written for the purpose of "giving...knowledge and discretion to the young" (Proverbs 1:4). What is the scene here, and what is the writer saying to his teenager in verses 10 and 15? What do you want to remember from this wise teaching?

✓ You'll love reading about the most famous friendship in the Bible, the beautiful relationship enjoyed between David and Jonathan, the son of King Saul, found in 1 Samuel 18:1-4; 19:1-6; and 20:1-42. It will take you a few minutes, but boy, is it worth it! Remember as you read the story of their friendship that King Saul was trying to murder David. We'll look at this friendship again in our next chapter, but for now, how did the friendship develop, and what was it based upon? What lessons in friendship can you take away from David and Jonathan?

11

A Heart That Is Loyal

A friend loves at all times....
There is a friend who sticks
closer than a brother.

PROVERBS 17:17; 18:24

It is such a joy to be the mother of two daughters. I have learned so much from my girls as we've gone through many of life's ups and downs together. And I can say that I *know*, from my own life as a teen and from witnessing, watching, worrying, and walking through the teen years of my daughters, that the whole area of friendships is vital...and volatile! It's vital in that everyone wants to have friends. And it's volatile in that friendships can blow up right in your face!

That's what one of my daughters found out...the hard way! When our family arrived back from the mission field, she was entering junior high school. And, because we had been gone, she had no friends. So as a family we began to pray for a friend for her. Well, soon we were all delighted when at last a friendship with another girl began to bud.

From a distance, it looked like all the ingredients were there for a godly "best-friend" relationship (like we learned about in the last chapter).

Well, one day after school my daughter ran through the front door at home wearing a necklace her new friend had given her. I'm sure you've seen one—the kind of necklace that has half a heart on it. It comes with two chains and two half-hearts, and each friend wears one. It's a friendship necklace. Needless to say, she was overjoyed! She had a friend! And her friend had gone so far as to purchase the two necklaces and to give my daughter one of them to wear, signifying their friendship. It appeared that our prayers had been answered.

But...can you guess the end of the story? It wasn't long before tensions set in, voices were raised, emotions ran high, and arguments began. And sure enough, the day arrived when one of these two "friends for life," these two "heart sisters," threw her half of the necklace at the other, and that friendship was shattered. It was over!...and we began to pray all over again.

Being a Friend

Have you had an experience like my daughter had? Then you know that finding a friend is not easy. No one ever said that it would be. And no one would ever say that being a friend is easy either. Being a friend—a friend like the scriptures at the beginning of this chapter describe, a friend who loves at all times and who sticks closer than a brother—is quite a challenge! But being such a friend is an important assignment God gives to you and me as women after His own heart.

From God's Word to Your Heart...

As always, God gives us our guidelines for life, and that includes our guidelines for being a loyal friend. As you read through these wise sayings from the Bible, formulate in your mind and heart what kind of friend you must be. Note, too, the things a friend does and does not do.

> *He who covers over an offense promotes love, but whoever repeats the matter separates close friends* (Proverbs 17:9).

> *A friend loves at all times, and a brother is born for adversity* (Proverbs 17:17).

> *A man of many companions may come to ruin, but there is a friend who sticks closer than a brother* (Proverbs 18:24).

> *Do not forsake your friend* (Proverbs 27:10).

Yes, But How?

Everyone has had experiences with flickering friendships that were short-lived, beginning quickly...and ending just as quickly. So how can we develop friendships that last? Obviously, we need to *find* the right friends to begin with. (That's what our last chapter was about.) But we also need to *be* the right kind of friend.

1. *Be loyal*—The most endearing and enduring quality between two friends is loyalty. We've all been hurt by a turncoat "friend." As we learned about David and Jonathan, true friends are equally loyal to each other. Their friendship wasn't one-sided or lopsided. Jonathan stood up to his father, King Saul, in defense of his friend David. And David kept his promise to Jonathan to look after his family members in the future. How loyal are you to your friends? Are you "a friend who sticks closer than a brother" (Proverbs 18:24)?

2. *Be understanding*—And don't keep score! Loyal love, according to 1 Corinthians 13:5, "keeps no record of wrongs." That means true friends don't get upset when a birthday is forgotten, when a phone call isn't returned, when time passes and there's no contact, when you don't get to touch base or sit together at church, when a friend spends time with someone else. Instead, true friends understand and support each other's commitments and responsibilities. They understand that family comes first, that

homework is important, that everyone is very busy. So pray for your friends, be understanding, and volunteer to help out when your friends are under pressure.

3. *Be respectful and sensitive*—For instance, when you call a friend, ask before you begin talking, "Is this a good time to talk, or do you want me to call back?" Also call and ask before you drop in or drop by for a visit. Don't forget...your friends have family responsibilities and relationships to take care of, chores, homework, piano practice, etc. Find out when the best time is for getting together.

4. *Be honest and be attentive*—One of the richest blessings of a solid friendship is honesty. The Bible says it this way—"Wounds from a friend can be trusted...and the pleasantness of one's friend springs from his earnest counsel" (Proverbs 27:6,9). Many people throughout your life will criticize you, but very few will be honest in their concern for you and speak to you face to face. That's one role of a true friend. You and a true friend should be committed to pulling each other along and pulling each other up toward God's goals for your lives as His young women. And don't forget, when your friend takes on this role to help you grow in an area where you need help, listen! Don't be proud. And don't be hurt. Thank your friend for caring enough to bring up a difficult subject (you can be sure it wasn't easy!), then

take it to the Lord in prayer. Examine your heart to see if what your friend said is true.

5. *Be careful with the opposite sex*—We'll devote time to this topic later in our book, but for now go back to the principles we learned from the Bible in the previous chapter. Be friendly to everyone, but be very cautious and take a *l-o-n-g* time when it comes to becoming friends with boys. The three things you'll really want to watch out for in your conduct and speech are being *too* friendly, being *too* flattering, and spending *too* much time talking. As I said, more later!

6. *Be witnessing in your encounters*—Those acquaintances in your life who are not Christians should be hearing you talk about Jesus, talk about God, talk about the Bible, talk about your church, and talk about your Bible study group. What happens when others hear you talk about these things (which, of course, are the most important things in your life, right?)? Those who hear you will possibly be put off by what you're saying and want nothing to do with you. Or maybe…just maybe!…they'll want to know more about your Savior, they'll want to go with you to church or to your youth group, and they'll want to do a Bible study with you. You see, *you* have the words of life—the gospel of Jesus Christ. And *you* have God's Word to give to all, "the holy Scriptures, which are able to make [others] wise for salvation

through faith in Christ Jesus" (2 Timothy 3:15). And God has placed these people in *your* life! So be bold for Jesus. And here's another huge benefit—when you speak up about your faith right away with a boy, it will let him know up front what you are all about. The boys in your life need to know right away that you are not interested in them if they are not passionate, active Christians.

7. *Be a constant encourager*—Let's go back a minute to the friendship between David and Jonathan. Their friendship, as we learned, was based on their love for God and on the things of the Lord. So how did they encourage one another? The Bible says that when it was evident David was targeted for murder, "Jonathan went to David...and helped him find strength in God" (1 Samuel 23:16). The best way to encourage your friends is in the Lord, with Scripture verses and through praying together. And when you give a compliment, be specific in your praise. Don't say, "Hey, that was great." Instead, say something like "I always appreciate the way you...." Take a few extra seconds to be specific. For instance, "I was watching you minister to that elderly woman, and you taught me a huge lesson by the way you...." Learn to praise conduct and character. It calls for a decision and some effort, but remember—your goal is to bring your friend along or up in her relationship with God. And with God, godly conduct and character count mightily!

8. *Be prioritizing your friendships*—You only have so much time in a day. So it's important that you identify who you are spending the bulk of your time with. And don't forget your family! They are the priority relationships God has given you. But after family, who are you spending time with, and how much? Is it those who pull you up and pull you along in your spiritual growth and walk with God? Is it those who help you to live out God's plan for your life with excellence? Who help you seek to set your heart and mind on things above, not on earthly things (Colossians 3:1-2)? Or is your time mostly spent with unbelievers or Christians who live on the edge or hang out on the fringe?

Don't get me wrong. Read number 6 again on pages 150-51. There's nothing wrong with giving of yourself to these acquaintances. But be sure they are not eating away your time, the time you could be studying the Word, being in a Bible study, being discipled, and being involved in a ministry at church. And be sure you are reaching out and ministering to these wonderful people. The best thing you can do for these friends is to find out (and that means listening!) the details of their lives, let them know how much you care for them and that you are praying for them, and continually ask them to come along with you to church or to your Bible study. Better yet, ask them to get together and have a Bible study *with* you! (And a word of caution here—you should *not* have a one-on-one Bible study with a boy. Leave that to your dad, an older brother, or a youth pastor! As I said, more on this later! But for now, trust me—don't do it!

9. *Be nurturing your friendships*—We never wake up in the morning and coldheartedly, calculatingly decide "I think I'll neglect my friends today." No, the neglect is more subtle. We just wake up in the morning and don't even *think* about our friends! Therefore, our friendships must be nurtured and developed. You and I have to make willful decisions about the keeping and growing of friendships— with both family and friends. And that takes time, care, and love…and maybe even a little money as you purchase a greeting card or small gift for a friend. The apostle Paul told his friends in Philippi, "I have you in my heart" (Philippians 1:7). Do you carry your friends in your heart?

10. *Be praying for your friends*—Dear one, we have no greater or finer (or more costly!) gift to give both our family and friends than to pray for them—faithfully, frequently, and fervently. Everyone struggles, and everyone faces trials and encounters crises. And we can be sure there are issues in our friends' lives that will never be shared with us. We'll never know all the battles that are being fought in another person's life. So, we pray.

And for what do we pray? Pray for your friends' spiritual growth, for their schoolwork, for their responsibilities and relationships at home with the members of their families for their involvement at church. And pray for others to come alongside them and encourage them, too. I especially love it when someone tells me exactly what they are praying for me. So be specific about what you are praying for them. And share specific Bible verses that you think will encourage them. You never know when the verse you share just might be the perfect "word that sustains the weary" and strengthens your friend to get through a tough day (Isaiah 50:4). And you never know when *you* just might be the true friend whose faithful, frequent, and fervent prayers help another to excel in greatness...or make it through a difficult life! So, dear friend, *pray* for your friends!

Heart Response

Is your heart moved? Mine is! As I said before, God intended us to have friends and to be a friend. You and I as women are social beings. We long to love and to be loved. That's the way God made us. So I want to encourage you (again!) in all your relationships—be the best friend anyone could ever have!

But I also want to caution you that friendships—true friendships—come with a price tag. And that price tag includes *time*. It takes time to find a friend. It takes time to be a friend. It takes time to remain a friend. And it takes time to pray for your friends.

So, precious friend, choose wisely. *Be* the best friend you can be to everyone…but *choose* wisely who your best friends will be. And how will you recognize those friends?

A friend will
strengthen you with her prayers,
bless you with her love, and
encourage you with her heart.[19]

Are you this kind of friend to others, a *loyal* friend?

*Things to Do Today to Develop
a Heart That Is Loyal*

♡ As you review the ten guidelines for loyal friendships, did you find an area where you are especially strong as a friend? What was it?

♡ As you review the ten guidelines for loyal friendships, did you find an area (or two!) where you need
improvement in the friendship department? What
was it, and what do you plan to do about it?

♡ What will you do to be a better encourager to each
of your friends tomorrow? This week?

Would You Like to Know More?
Check It Out

✓ Read 1 Corinthians 13:4-8. List the marks of loyal love found in these few verses. As you think about the level of your love for your friends, how would you rate yourself, and why? Go a step further and write out what you plan to do to get a better grade. (And don't forget to ask God for His help!)

✓ What do these scenarios teach us about friendships? Read Psalm 41:9; Psalm 55:12-14; Matthew 26:50; Acts 15:36-41. As you read, note what people were involved and any details mentioned. What conclusions can you draw about friends and friendships?

✓ Paul had a passion for prayer and for praying for his friends. Read the content of these prayers: Philippians 1:9-11; Colossians 1:9-12; Ephesians 3:14-19. Do you need to beef up your prayers for your friends? (Or do you perhaps need to beef up your prayer life, period?) What changes and improvements will you make to become a better friend, a woman after God's own heart who prays for her friends?

12

A Heart That Grows

*And Jesus grew in wisdom and stature,
and in favor with God and men.*

LUKE 2:52

It may be hard for you to believe, but I used to sit exactly where you're sitting right now—sitting for hours on end in classrooms at school and in my room at home at night for even more hours of homework. In fact, I can say that I probably spent *more* hours at school and at school work than you do. Why? Because both my parents were schoolteachers—which meant that every day of my life I went to the school where my mother taught or to the school where my father taught! I got to school early (and sat in their empty classrooms studying), and I stayed at school late (sitting in their empty classrooms doing homework). *Then* I got to go home...and put in even more time on my homework!

Yes, my parents definitely put a premium on education. So much so that they worked long and hard—even teaching nights and summers—to put all four of their children through college. For this I am most thankful!

But I have to admit that I wondered almost daily all through junior high and high school and even college, *Why?!* Why was all this school work so important? I could understand why it was important for my three brothers. But me? I mean, wasn't I supposed to grow up, meet a great guy, get married, and have a family?

Why Grow? Why Learn? Why Go to School?

What I've just expressed above is pretty much how my thoughts went all the way through my 16-plus years of schooling, right up until I graduated from the University of Oklahoma. And sure enough, I did meet a great guy (Jim), get married, and have a family. And believe me, *that's* when I really had my eyes opened to the value of my education! (And please realize that when I say *education* I'm not talking about college. No, I'm talking about *all* schooling—the kind of education you are getting right now by going to school—whether on a campus or at home, and as you faithfully do your homework assignments.)

Well, dear heart, I can only tell you today that I wish my parents were still here to hear me tell them one more time, "Thank you for my education!" I can't tell you how many times in the passing decades I've spoken these words to them.

I say this because these many years later—after being a wife and homemaker for 38 years and after raising two daughters—I know that the things I learned in school and the skills, habits, and character qualities I obtained because of the work and grind of school equipped me for my roles as wife, mother, and homemaker. I was able to learn how to fulfill these God-assigned roles because I already knew from my time spent being a student how to learn, to grow, to read, to organize, to schedule, to study, and to manage projects. I had learned how to acquire knowledge. And I had learned how to complete and finish work assignments.

Therefore, over the years and through the seasons of my life, I've been able to tackle daily problems and learn new skills. The know-how achieved through my years of going to school has also enabled me to minister, whether taking on the challenge of teaching a Sunday school class of little ones or doing research and creating a curriculum for a large women's Bible study, as well as teaching the study. And I am still learning new things, as God has given me a fresh and different (and stretching!) ministry of writing books for Christian women.

I truly love and enjoy everything I do and everything I've done. For instance, I love being a homemaker. Home-making is an art, and as a homemaker I have the privilege of expressing and developing all my talents in my little place called home. I get to build...beautify...organize... create...fuss...express myself. I get to read and study and grow and master nutrition, finances, horticulture, design, and wardrobe. And I love being a mother. I loved teaching and training my children and giving their precious lives a bent toward God. And now I love passing on the truth about Jesus to yet another generation, to my grandchildren.

But, my dear young woman after God's own heart, here's the point I'm trying to make—to do all this, or to do whatever God is asking of you (and me), means that you've got to be a woman who is continuing to grow. You've got to be dedicated, organized, and a woman of purpose.

✎ *From God's Word to Your Heart...*

The Bible is filled with examples of God's servants who had to learn before they could lead. Moses, Daniel, Jesus, Paul—all had years of training and schooling. Even the women of the early church were taught by those older than they were (Titus 2:3-5). As you read these scriptures, what comes to your mind regarding the importance of all education and learning and your daily schoolwork?

> *Let the wise listen and add to their learning, and let the discerning get guidance* (Proverbs 1:5).

> *For the LORD gives wisdom, and from his mouth come knowledge and understanding* (Proverbs 2:6).

> *And Jesus grew in wisdom and stature, and in favor with God and men* (Luke 2:52).

Whatever you do, work at it with all your heart, as working for the Lord, not for men (Colossians 3:23).

But grow in the grace and knowledge of our Lord and Savior Jesus Christ (2 Peter 3:18).

Yes, But How?

Are you catching on? Catching a glimpse of God's plan for you to learn and grow? Catching a vision of why, as you prepare for a lifetime of serving God and others, your school work is an important part of your life?

That's my prayer for you. And here are some actions you can take that will hopefully motivate you even further to develop a heart that grows.

1. *Accept*—You need to accept that God is calling you to follow the normal course of events in your life. And that normal course includes your schooling. In God's economy, everything is "done in a fitting and orderly way" (1 Corinthians 14:40). You cannot skip over any part of life that is unpleasant, that isn't fun. Just think about Jesus. We've already noted in our book that Jesus—God in flesh(!)—lived at home

and was subject to His parents' authority. But He also "grew in wisdom and stature, and in favor with God and men" (Luke 2:52). Nothing and no normal phase was omitted from Jesus' life.

Just as God the Father had a plan for Jesus' life, He has a plan for yours, too. And the Father's plan includes the normal process of developing mentally by going to school and maturing through the knowledge and experience gained in the process. You gain the treasure of education when you accept that your schooling is God's will for your life.

2. *Embrace*—You also need to embrace God's plan for academic growth. Yes, you prepare spiritually for the future, but you also prepare academically for your future.

Here's the way it is—you have your whole life in front of you. You don't know yet what God has planned for you, but you prepare for a life of serving Him and others. You don't know whether you're preparing to serve God by working on the home-front as a wife, mother, and homemaker, by working on the mission field, or by working at a job. Any one of these "professions" will be demanding and require years of focused preparation. So I urge you to embrace this aspect of your life, this aspect of preparing by schooling. Accept it with great excitement, anticipation, and prayer!

3. *Excel*—God wants you to excel at everything you do. In His Word He tells us, "Whatever you do, work at it with all your heart, as working for the Lord, not for men" (Colossians 3:23). And that "work" for you as a young person includes your school work. Therefore you should "work at it with all your heart," heartily and hard! Why? So you can develop habits and skills of excellence for managing your life today and for all of your future. The disciplines acquired by excellence will give you the greatest education of all—a life of wisdom. Wisdom—not academic excellence or good grades or a bushel of knowledge, but wisdom—is your goal as a Christian. As Solomon, the wisest person in Old Testament times, wrote, "Wisdom is supreme; therefore get wisdom" (Proverbs 4:7).

And here's another benefit of doing the best work you can—it gives you credibility with your peers. I'm not talking about being popular. Being a strong Christian with moral convictions is difficult on the school campus and makes you stand out as different. No, popularity is not to be your goal. But if you are "the best" at your schoolwork, people will be interested in knowing more about you and your life. They may still think you're "weird," but they will respect you and your standards for excellence and your accomplishments, which then may open the door for you to share about your faith in Christ.

4. *Examine*—You must develop discernment in order to examine what is being taught in your classrooms. And your ability to discern truth from ungodly teaching will be in direct proportion to the wisdom you have gained from your study of the Bible, through prayer, and through wise counsel (Proverbs 1:5). So if you attend a public school, there will be times when a teacher will teach something you as a Christian don't believe. (I'm sure this has already happened to you!) And even if you attend a Christian school, there may be times when a teacher will teach something different from what your church or parents or pastor teaches. What can you do at such times? Here's a preliminary checklist of do's and don'ts:

- Do ask for clarification.

- Do ask your parents' advice.

- Do follow your parents' advice.

- Do ask your pastor, if your parents aren't able to help.

- Do pray about the situation and for wisdom.

- Don't overreact and cause a scene.

- Don't confront the teacher in the classroom.

- Don't show disrespect for the teacher's position of authority.

Combining all the *do's* and *don'ts,* do make sure you respond with Christian love and with respect for your teacher.

5. *Exemplify*—You need to exemplify Christ and uphold the standard He sets in the Bible for your conduct on your school campus. For instance, do you dress like everyone else at school? If someone were to look down the crowded halls of your school, would you blend in with the crowd? If someone new arrived on your campus and followed you around for a few days, would they say that you adhered to different beliefs and values than most of the other kids in the school? If you are modeling Jesus Christ at your school, then there will be a noticeable difference between you and the other students. Your days and years spent at school are the training ground for living the Christian life. You must decide who you are living to please—your friends?...or your friend Jesus?

And one more thought before we close this most important chapter—if you are having a hard time living for Christ at school, then you will have a hard time living for Christ in the world. How you model Christlikeness at school today is how you will more than likely model Christ in the future when you are an adult. I've said this before, but I simply must say it again—what you will be tomorrow, you are becoming today. So live for Christ today and, my friend, you will live for Christ tomorrow.

I hope you enjoyed this chapter. I know I did. It was my opportunity and delight to have a heart-to-heart time with you. As I said, I love being a woman after God's own heart—every aspect of it! And I so desire for you to love it, too!

To me, being a woman is like being a flower. As the seasons of life pass from one to the next, God presents new roles for us to take on, new things for us to learn, and new challenges for us to conquer. As these challenges arrive, we call upon God's great grace and tackle them full-on. We put God's wisdom and our education to use. We tap into all the strong character traits and solid learning skills gained through our hours and days and years spent in school. And we draw upon God and His Holy Spirit to strengthen us and help us walk along life's way. And then, through this process of growth, the flower of our life develops, blossoms, blooms, and flourishes as we serve God in each and every place where He plants us. The days pass. The decades pass. The flower grows. And then one day we meet our Lord face to face. And it is then, dear one, that we present ourselves to Him, in full bloom.

Being a Christian woman is a wonderful life! So make sure yours is a heart that is growing so you can enjoy the journey!

*Things to Do Today to Develop
a Heart That Grows*

♡ Look at your schedule for this past week and esti-
mate the number of hours you spent in these three
categories: time goofing off, time with friends, and
time on homework. What does your schedule reveal?
Are there any changes called for?

♡ How would you evaluate your Christian presence on
your school campus? Are you a "secret agent" for
Christ? Or are you a "special agent" for Christ? Please
explain your answer. Then ask a Christian friend at
your school to pray for your witness to be loud and
bold, and to hold you accountable. (P.S., you might
want to do the same for her!)

♡ Where does the thermometer of your heart's commitment register on the "attitude scale" when it comes to school and your schoolwork? How will you turn up the heat of your heart in this most important area of life?

Would You Like to Know More?
Check It Out

✓ Read Daniel 1:1-7 and 17-20. Describe the process of learning for the teen Daniel and his three friends. How does their experience motivate you in your own schooling?

✓ Read Luke 2:41-49. What do Jesus' younger years teach you about your own developmental process?

✓ Gamaliel was one of the most prominent teachers of his day. Read Acts 5:34. Who was Gamaliel's famous student, according to Acts 22:3? Again, what example is being set for you?

✓ Read Titus 2:3-5. Besides the teaching you receive in the school classroom, what further training should you have for the future, according to verses 4 and 5? Who is helping you to grow in some of these areas? Or who *could* help you if you asked?

13

A Heart That Serves

Always give yourselves fully to the work of the Lord, because…your labor in the Lord is not in vain.

1 CORINTHIANS 15:58

Everyone has a hero or two. And an amazing thing about heroes is that most of them have hearts that serve. Joan of Arc loved God, served God, and fought valiantly as she served others. Do you know her story?

Joan of Arc was a French peasant who lived in the thirteenth century. When France was occupied by the English, she convinced the king to put her at the head of 10,000 troops. She rallied the French forces to liberate France and has been since dubbed "The Maid of Orleans," heroine of France. Joan of Arc couldn't read or write, but she cared deeply and she prayed passionately. And here's the shocker—Joan of Arc was 19 when she died. She was a teenager! To this day this teenage woman is considered to be a national heroine of France. As she prepared for death, Joan of Arc prayed, "I shall only last a year; use me as You can." Hers was a heart committed to serving others to the very end.

Well, my young friend, God wants you and me to have hearts that serve, too. He has given us everything we need for living our lives in a godly way (2 Peter 1:3), He has blessed us with every spiritual blessing (Ephesians 1:3), and He has gifted us spiritually to serve others in the church (1 Corinthians 12:7). It's like this—God has given us everything we will ever need in life, and He expects us to, in turn, reach out and share what we have with others, to help better the lives of others.

We've talked about our roles with family, friends, and those who do not know our Jesus. But now it's time to talk about our responsibilities to other Christians. So let's see how it is that God wants us to serve one another in the church.

Learn to Reach Out

Again and again Jesus tells us to give—to give to everyone (Luke 6:30), and to give without expecting to get anything back (verse 35), to give in the generous way God, who is kind to the ungrateful and wicked, gives (verse 35), and to care for others by giving (verse 38). So how can you and I go about giving in this way? How can we learn to let our hearts overflow with care for others? How can we begin to reach out and serve others? Here are a few ideas:

- *Be there*—When it comes to reaching out to others in ministry, remember that you must first be there. In order to serve others in the church, you must be there. So make your attendance at church and at your youth activities a high priority.

And here's another benefit to being there—your very presence is a source of comfort and help to others. You may not always know exactly what to say or do, but you can be there. So if someone is suffering, you can at least go up to her and speak to her, stand beside her, talk to her, and put your arm around her shoulder. But first you must be there!

- *Be a giver*—The Bible says "do not withhold good from those who deserve it, when it is in your power to act" (Proverbs 3:27). So open your heart and give. Give the smile, the greeting, the interested question, the touch, and the hug. These are small things that mean a lot to others.

- *Be bold*—By this I mean that when God puts someone in your path who is suffering or hurting, don't think, "I've got to go find someone to help her. I've got to go find Pastor." No, you be bold. First reach out to that person, find out what the need is, and *then* go find Pastor or someone else to help if you need to. Maybe all the person needs is a shoulder to cry on or someone to pray with her. That someone can be you!

- *Be generous*—And by this I mean not only with money and things, but with praise, encouragement, thanks, a greeting, kindness, good deeds, and notes of appreciation. You and I can *choose* to give these tiny blessings that cost us so little and mean so much to others, or we can choose *not* to give them. So when someone shares something difficult from her life in your Bible study group, tell her that you appreciated what she had to say...and that you appreciate her. Thank your Bible study leader for the lesson and for her hard work. Go another step and tell her what meant the most to you from the lesson, what you learned. Tell those who organized your church group outing or camp or who opened their homes to your group that you are thankful for their hard work.

Learn to Look Out

Do you know the story in the Bible of the shepherd who had 100 sheep and discovered that one was missing (Luke 15:1-7)? Well, what amazes me is that the shepherd dropped everything and went looking for that one sheep. And what amazes me even more is that that's the way God cares for you and me. And here's something else that's amazing—God expects you and me to care for others in this same way! So here are a few tips on learning to look out.

- *Develop a "bountiful eye"*—The Bible says that "he who has a bountiful eye will be blessed" (Proverbs 22:9 KJV). I think of a bountiful eye as being like the eyes of the Lord, which "run" and "range throughout the earth to strengthen those whose hearts are fully committed to him" (2 Chronicles 16:9). So here's what I do. Whenever I go out in public, I intentionally look for wounded sheep.

And believe me, they are everywhere! I've found women crying in the restroom at church, sitting on a planter on the patio weeping, even standing behind the prayer room door at church sobbing their eyes out. When you find someone in need...then what?

- *Be direct*—I've had to learn (yes, *learn!*) to be direct and to reach out to hurting people. It's not always easy, but it's the right thing to do.

One night at church I was sitting beside a stranger, a visitor to our church. Well, this woman bawled through the entire evening. I could hardly wait for my pastor to say "amen" so I could turn to her and say, "Is there *anything* I can do for you? Do you want to talk? Can I pray with you? Can I get you something?" Well, my friend, hers was a spiritual need. She needed the Savior...and that was the night she became a Christian! God was working in her heart and He used me in a small way to help her. Praise Him!

Go to Give

I'm so happy to share with you some words that have changed my life. They are from missionary and martyr Jim Elliot, who once said,

> Wherever you are, be all there.
> Live to the hilt every situation
> you believe to be the
> will of God.[20]

I try to keep these words in mind wherever I am and whatever I'm doing (like writing this book right now while the sun is shining and the gorgeous weather outdoors is trying to woo me away from my computer!). But I especially try to keep these words in mind whenever I attend any church or ministry event. I go expecting God to use me. And, of course, I want to encourage you to do the same. How?

- *Be all there*—Before I go to any event, I pray that I will go to give. I pray to reach out, to look out, to be direct, to withhold nothing. Then, as I go, I put all other thoughts on hold. While I'm at Bible study, I don't think about what I'm going to do when I get home. And during my pastor's message I don't plan my week and worry about my to-do list. Plus, I don't want to be concerned about what happened before I got there or what will happen after the event. I want to be all there!

- *Live to the hilt!*—Not only do I want to be all there, but I want to also live each moment to the hilt! My philosophy is that as long as I'm there, as long as I'm giving an evening or a morning to be at a church event or at the worship service, I want to give totally. I want to reach out to as many sheep as I can, to minister to as many people as I can and in as many ways as I can. And, dear one, I (of course again!) want that for you, too, so that *you* can be used by God to touch the lives of others, and so that the lives of others can be bettered by your great heart that serves!

- *Divide and conquer*—This is a hard one…but I want you to agree with your closest girlfriends *not* to sit together, walk together, share together, or visit while you're at church. Instead I want you and your group to divide and conquer. Here's what will happen if you do this. You came to give, right? So how can you give to others if you are constantly with your best friends? You can talk to them any time at school or on the phone or over at your house or theirs. But what about the stranger, the first-time visitor who's all alone at church and doesn't know anyone? And what about those who are hurting, who are lonely, who had a rough time at home before they came to church (or maybe who have a rough time at home *all the time!)?* Your closest friends have open access to you and your time. They have plenty of one-on-one time with you in private. So why should they have your *public* time too? You can talk and get together later. So make a pact to divide and conquer. If you find you are gravitating toward each other, say, "Come on! Let's go touch some sheep!"

Give in Prayer

Hmmm. Here we are again—back to prayer. We began our book with prayer, and over and over again we keep returning to it. But by now you and I both realize that that's what a woman after God's own heart is all about. She is a pray-er! So pray, dear one! Pray for others. Pray for your pastor and those who work at the church. Pray for your youth leader. If he or she is married, pray for the spouse and family. Pray for your church's missionaries. Pray for others to come to Christ. Prayer is a ministry, a ministry that makes a huge difference in people's lives. So do whatever it takes to develop your prayer life. How? As we learned earlier...

- *Determine a time*—make sure you have a time (*your* time) for prayer.

- *Determine a place*—make sure you have a place (*your* place) for prayer.

- *Determine a plan*—make sure you have a plan for organizing your ministry of prayer (a notebook, a list, a journal). And while you're at it, set up a plan for exactly what days you want to pray for which people. Some people (like your family and friends) you'll want to pray for every day. And you'll want to choose a specific day of the week to pray for others (like your pastors and missionaries and teachers at school). Put all this information in your master plan for prayer.

Dear sister after God's own heart, there's one more thing I want to share as you and I dream of developing hearts that serve. As we look out and reach out and give and serve, as we let God use us in these small ways, something wonderful happens—you and I are blessed beyond what we can imagine. As we take these small but sometimes difficult steps and serve others, we grow a character that desires to look out, reach out, give, and serve even more. And that, my friend, is the character of a hero! A hero has a heart that serves others.

✎ *From God's Word to Your Heart...*

I know I've shared a lot of scriptures as we've made our way through this chapter, but now I want you to look at some more. Whisper a prayer to God to use His Word in your heart to transform it into a heart that loves His people and serves them selflessly and compassionately. As you read, ask your heart, "How can I become a better servant to the people of God?"

> *Whoever wants to become great among you must be your servant, and whoever wants to be first must be your slave—just as the Son of Man did not come to be served, but to serve, and to give his life as a ransom for many* (Matthew 20:26-28).

> *Always give yourselves fully to the work of the Lord, because you know that your labor in the Lord is not in vain* (1 Corinthians 15:58).

> *Serve one another in love* (Galatians 5:13).

Serve wholeheartedly, as if you were serving the Lord, not men (Ephesians 6:7).

And pray in the Spirit on all occasions with all kinds of prayers and requests. With this in mind, be alert and always keep on praying for all the saints (Ephesians 6:18).

We began this chapter talking about heroes. What makes a person a hero? A person doesn't become a hero because he or she decides to. No, a hero is born when some incident occurs, and he or she answers the call with a heroic act. A hero is just an ordinary person who, on one day, with one act, does the extraordinary. Or a hero could be someone just like you—a young person who serves others faithfully.

When I think of someone who had a heart that cared and served, I can't help but think of one particular woman in the Old Testament. You can read her story for yourself (see 2 Kings 4:8-10), but for now, let me give you the condensed version. This nameless woman, who is referred to as "the Shunammite" in the Bible, saw that the prophet Elisha had no place to stay when he came to her town on his preaching tours. So this dear woman asked her husband if they could build a small room on their roof for the prophet to stay in when he came to town.

So what did the Shunammite do that was so great? So heroic? She did what you and I *could* do and *should* do— She *looked out* and saw a need, she *reached out* and extended a helping hand, and she *gave out* of a heart of love for another person.

Dear young sister, God has given us an example in this woman and her actions (and her heart). We, too, should be looking out and reaching out and extending a helping hand to those around us. The Shunammite woman will never be found on any list of heroes. But we can be sure that every time God's weary prophet Elisha entered that little room on the top of her house, the Shunammite was a hero in his eyes.

You can be a hero, too. How? By following the advice of the apostle Paul, who said, "as we have opportunity, let us do good to all people, especially to those who belong to the family of believers" (Galatians 6:10). Begin with goodness. And then stand back as God grows in you a heart that serves. The instructions are simple (read them below). However, the follow-through will take a lifetime!

> Do all the good you can,
> by all the means you can,
> in all the ways you can,
> in all the places you can,
> at all the times you can,
> to all the people you can,
> as long as ever you can.[21]

Things to Do Today to Develop a Heart That Serves

♡ As you are finishing this chapter, what church event is next on your calendar? How can you put the principles you've just learned about developing a heart that serves into action?

♡ Review again the principles from this chapter about serving others. Then list three things you can definitely do to serve those in your church. Now, who can you call for some accountability as you pray to follow through on your good intentions?

♡ Just for today...do all the good you can, by all the means you can, in all the ways you can, in all the places you can, at all the times you can, to all the people you can.

Would You Like to Know More?
Check It Out

✓ Read now the story of the Shunammite woman in 2 Kings 4:8-10. What principles for serving others did she live out? How does she set a good example for you in your service to others?

✓ For a look at another hero, read about Dorcas in Acts 9:36-41. What principles for serving others did she live out? How does she set a good example for you in your service to others?

✓ The Bible teaches that every Christian has been given *spiritual gifts* "for the common good" of those in the church (1 Corinthians 12:7). According to 1 Peter 4:9-11, what are some of these spiritual gifts that you can use in your church? How can you be faithful to serve other believers "for the common good"?

✓ Jesus, of course, is God's ultimate example of a heart that serves. Prayerfully read Philippians 2:3-8. How did Jesus serve others (verses 5-8)? And what does the apostle Paul say you should do to develop a heart that serves (verses 3-4)?

14

A Heart Marked by Purity

*An unmarried woman or virgin is
concerned about the Lord's affairs:
Her aim is to be devoted to the Lord
in both body and spirit.*

1 CORINTHIANS 7:34

As I interact with women of all ages and listen to their hearts, answer their letters, and hold their hands as they sob and share their problems and regrets, believe me, this whole area of purity ranks right at the top. It's a big issue for every woman.

Before we dive into this all-important area of your life, I hope and pray you realize that all that's gone before this chapter in this book is foundational to this issue of purity of body, soul, and spirit. Your love for God and your family, coupled with your obedience to God and to your parents, is meant to make you whole and surround you with loving relationships that build lasting godly character in you. What an advantage you possess if these basic elements of purity are present in your life!

I know that whole books have been written on the subjects of purity, dating, and premarital relationships. And depending on your age and your situation, you may want to read some of them. But for my purpose of presenting an overview of the priority areas of your life as a young Christian woman, I want to give you a brief, to-the-point summary or checklist. And as you read, keep this in mind—God has given you His Word, your church, and your parents to walk you through (and walk *with* you through!) the teen years of your life. And He has also given you the power of the Holy Spirit to enable you to stay pure, to resist the flesh, and to fortify you with His self-control (Galatians 5:22-23).

A Few Words About Purity

Like all the areas of your life, God expects you to oversee and manage your purity. God has entrusted you with this most precious possession—your purity. And purity must be maintained on all levels. For instance...

- Your physical purity is something very special and should be preserved at all cost.

- Your mental purity is where it all starts. What you think greatly determines how you behave.

- Your spiritual purity deals with your heart. The heart of a woman after God's own heart is a pure heart, a heart that desires to be pure.

God makes it very clear in the Bible that He wants His women to be pure. In fact, in Titus 2:3-5, God specifically instructs the older women in the church and in the faith to teach and train the younger women "to be…pure" (verse 5). It amazes me that there are only six topics listed that these older saints are to teach to their younger sisters in the Lord, and *purity* is one of them. That, my friend, most definitely ranks purity high on God's list for you and me!

So a woman after God's own heart—no matter what her age, whether a preteen, a teen, a collegian, a career woman, a young wife and mom, a middle-aged woman, or senior saint—pays close attention to purity. Indeed, God calls *all* Christians to be pure and to keep themselves pure.

The word "pure" (Titus 2:5) is translated in different versions of the Bible as "chaste" and "pure-minded." And if you look up the word "pure" in your dictionary, you'll discover that it means to be without stain, to be free from pollution, to be clean, and to be innocent and guiltless.

✎ *From God's Word to Your Heart…*

Let's pause a minute and take these scriptures to heart. As we head into this rubber-meets-the-road topic, pray as you read the following verses. Pray that God would sear them into the tender flesh of your heart (Proverbs 3:3). Pray that God's Holy Spirit and God's Holy Word would impress upon you the changes you must make regarding your own purity and your view of the importance of your purity. Pray about the instruction each scripture sends to your heart about your purity.

Keep yourself pure (1 Timothy 5:22).

Finally, brothers, whatever is…pure…think about such things (Philippians 4:8).

Flee the evil desires of youth, and pursue righteousness, faith, love and peace, along with those who call on the Lord out of a pure heart (2 Timothy 2:22).

To the pure, all things are pure (Titus 1:15).

A Word About Dating

I'm sure you're aware that a raging battle is going on in Christian circles about the whole area of dating—do you or don't you date? Should you or shouldn't you date? If yes, at what age? And do you call it *dating* or *courting?* And if you do go on a date, do you go as a couple or in a group? On and on the discussions go.

At the time our two daughters were growing up, every family was pretty much on its own to decide its own standards and guidelines. There were few, if any, books written on the subject of dating. Everyone—both the teenagers and their parents—was left to themselves to fumble their way through the teen years. With much prayer and consultation with older, wiser parents, my husband, Jim, as the head of our household, laid out these three standards for our girls.

- There would be no dates or even discussions of dates until our girls were 16.

- After 16 there would still be no dates, but Katherine and Courtney could go to special events, such as the annual high school banquet, with a boy and a few other couples *if* that boy asked Jim first.

- After graduation from high school the girls could go out with a guy *if* he called Jim (even long distance) to ask for permission. This applied even if it was only to get a Coke.

I don't know how this sounds to you (I can only imagine!), but these three standards protected our daughters from dealing with unnecessary and premature emotions, from peer pressure, and from the wrong kind of young men. (And, by the way, our daughters have continued to thank us for these guidelines ever since!)

That's the way it was in our family with our teenage daughters. Now, what will it be for you? Why not set a high standard? Why not...

- *Choose* not to date all the way through high school. There's a 99 percent chance that any boy you date before you reach marriageable age will *not* be your future mate! (Think about that!) So what's the point of dating? Be aware that dating is an emotional roller coaster that can leave you sick after each ride.

- *Choose* to concentrate on group activities, preferably church activities. Interact with the young men there.

- *Choose* to make sure your family is involved and gets to know any boy friends well.

- *Choose* to remain morally pure no matter what. You must make this choice before you begin dating and before each date you go on, whatever your age.

I can almost hear you wondering, "But what if I'm already dating?" Well, my dear friend, read on! And especially note what I say about being around the right kind of friends, whether male or female. You want to make sure you are dating a young man who desires to follow God's heart—and that means a young man who is an active Christian, a young man whose love for God keeps him committed to God's command for purity in his life...and yours, too! Christ must have authority in his life just as Christ has authority in your life. And his heart, like yours, must be set on obeying God's plan for your purity and his.

Now, let's learn more about the marks of a young man after God's own heart!

A Word About Boys

It's a given that you will be around boys. But, I repeat(!), by all means, make sure the boys you are around are vibrant active Christians! Surround yourself with the kind of friends—male or female—who pull you along in your spiritual growth and pull you up toward godliness. Starting now, use the Bible's highest standards for a Christian man as your guideline for guys. These standards are found in 1 Timothy 3 and Titus 1, but in a nutshell they call for a man of God to be blameless in character and godly in conduct. This standard is high. That's because it's *God's* standard, not man's standard. Dear one, God desires the best from *you*, and you should desire the best in a young man. Don't settle for anyone less than the best—a man after God's own heart!

A Word About Your Dress

I want to share two things in this area of dress. First, I want you to know what the Bible says about your dress (and it says it in one word!)—it's to be *modest* (1 Timothy 2:9).

But second, I want you to hear what a young man has to say about your dress. His name is Jason Perry of the Christian music group Plus One. Jim and I were on a panel with Jason that answered questions about dating—questions asked by representatives of a large Christian bookselling chain. In his book *You Are Not Your Own*, Jason has this to say about your dress:

> When I see girls dressed [in] a suggestive way, I not only turn my head away, but I pray for them. Obviously, there's a deeper issue—they are looking for affirmation in the wrong ways. My question is, Is that how you want guys to see you—as a sex object? Or would you rather have a guy know you and care for you because of your character, not just your outward beauty?
>
> I love seeing girls who dress in a way that is not disrespectful to themselves. Girls, God tells us to be holy and pure with our bodies. Even though our culture tells you it's OK to wear clothing that is sexy or almost nonexistent, I want to challenge you to walk a different road. There are plenty of ways to be hip and trendy and to look great without being seductive or flirtatious.[22]

Now, my friend, let's both agree "to walk a different road" when it comes to our dress. Let's be holy and pure and modest in our dress.

A Word About Your Mind

Where do impure thoughts and interests come from? Well, it's obvious they come from the flesh (Galatians 5:19)! But where else? They come from the world, from what we see on TV and in movies, from what we read in magazines and in books, and from what we hear from others. Such information is then planted in our minds.

Beloved, God calls you and me as His women to obliterate impure thoughts from our minds. What does He say to think on instead of sensuous and worldly thoughts? "Whatever is *pure*...think about such things" (Philippians 4:8)! God also tells us that our impure thoughts reveal an impure heart—"Out of the *heart* come evil thoughts...adultery, sexual immorality" (Matthew 15:19). Did you catch it? Our thoughts are a matter of the *heart!* So do a quick heart check—what do you think about? And what do you think about others? Is it pure? Then heed God's advice:

> *How can a young man [or woman] keep his way pure? By living according to your word. I seek you with all my* heart; *do not let me stray from your commands. I have hidden your word in my* heart *that I might not sin against you* (Psalm 119:9-11).

A Word About Your Mouth

And here's another lesson about purity—God's Word says "Do not let any unwholesome talk come out of your mouths." What are we to talk about instead? That which "is helpful for building others up" (Ephesians 4:29). Whether we acknowledge it or not, what we allow ourselves to think will sooner or later be expressed by our mouths. Our thoughts lead to words. It's just as Jesus said, "Out of the overflow of the *heart* the mouth speaks" (Matthew 12:34). (Did you catch it again—our speech is also a matter of the heart!) To sum up what we are learning, I immediately think of these simple words of caution:

> Be careful, little eyes, what you see,
> Be careful, little ears, what you hear,
> Be careful, little mind, what you think,
> Be careful, little mouth, what you say,
> If you want to grow.

A Word About Your Parents

If being a teenager is difficult, then you've got to realize that being the *parent* of a teenager is difficult, too. But remember that no one knows you better, loves you more, or wants your best more than your parents. That's why I'll say it again—heed their guidelines when it comes to your relationships and their standards for your purity, and desire their approval of your friends of both sexes and your activities.

A Word About Your Standards

On this matter I have a very brief word for you—*set* your standards, and set them *high!* When my daughters were in grade school, Jim asked them to write down the kind of man they thought God wanted them to marry. Then, as the years passed, and cute, cool, popular guys began to flow through their lives, Jim would get out the lists the girls had written and ask, "Does this guy meet your standards?" I urge you to do the same thing. As I said, *set* your standards, and set them *high!* (And while you're at it, set standards for yourself, for the kind of godly woman this godly man would want for a wife!)

A Word About Your Body

Your physical purity is important to God. Why? Because…

- Your body is a temple—"Do you not know that your body is a temple of the Holy Spirit, who is in you?" (1 Corinthians 6:19).

- Your body is not your own—"You are not your own" (1 Corinthians 6:19).

- Your body is bought with a price—"You were bought at a price" (1 Corinthians 6:20). And what was that price? "The precious blood of Christ" (1 Peter 1:19).

- Your body is to honor and glorify God—"Honor God with your body" (1 Corinthians 6:20). Therefore, "it is God's will that you should be sanctified; that you should avoid sexual immorality; that each of you should learn to control his own body in a way that is holy and honorable, not in passionate lust" (1 Thessalonians 4:3-5).

A Word About Your Friends

Don't forget to choose your friends wisely! They will make all the difference in the world in your purity. God's Word says you are to "pursue righteousness, faith, love and peace, along with those who call on the Lord out of a pure heart" (2 Timothy 2:22). Remember…no friends is better than the wrong friends!

A Word About the World

The Bible urges you and me as His cherished women, "Do not conform any longer to the pattern of this world" (Romans 12:2)! It's soooo easy for us to be conformed to the standards and morals of our society. Therefore…

- You must be "transformed by the renewing of your mind" (Romans 12:2).

- You must not "love the world or anything in the world" (1 John 2:15).

- You must "flee the evil desires of youth" (2 Timothy 2:22).

- You must not pattern our lives after those "who do not know God" (1 Thessalonians 4:5).

- You must remember that you are *in* the world, but not *of* the world (John 17:14,16).

A Word About Your Future

God has a plan for your life, even for your life right now as a young single woman. What is it?

An unmarried woman or virgin is concerned about the Lord's affairs: Her aim is to be devoted to the Lord in both body and spirit (1 Corinthians 7:34).

God's plan for you is that you keep yourself pure in body and mind and that you serve Him. *God* is to be the consuming priority of your life. You are His child. Therefore you are to live for Him and according to His Word. You are to live the way *He* wants you to live. And not only are you to keep yourself pure in body and in mind for God *now* as a single, but you are also to keep yourself pure in body and in mind for a future husband, if marriage is God's will for your future.

A Word About Your Looks

We couldn't have a book for women and not say something about our looks, could we? However, it's interesting that the Bible contains very little about our outward appearance. Perhaps that's because the Bible is a spiritual book and focuses our attention on the "inner" man and woman (2 Corinthians 4:16).

But there are definite ways you and I can take care of our looks. And God does comment on the outward appearance of some of the women of the Bible. For instance...

- Sarah was called a beautiful woman by her husband Abraham (Genesis 12:11).

- Both Rebekah and Rachel were described as beautiful of form and face (Genesis 24:16 and 29:17).

- The exquisite Esther took care of her appearance, dressed with care, and "won the favor of everyone who saw her" (Esther 2:15).

- We don't know what the Proverbs 31 woman looked like, but we do know that her clothes were special—fine silk and purple (Proverbs 31:22).

It seems clear that beauty and the care of your appearance has a place in your daily life. Don't worry so much about what you look like. You look exactly as God meant you to look (Psalm 139:14). But you can make an effort in the care of your appearance. So fix up…a little! Make up…a little! Dress up…a little! Shape up…a little! Others will be most grateful.

But never forget these words from the Bible: "Charm is deceptive, and beauty is fleeting; but a woman who fears the LORD is to be praised" (Proverbs 31:30). Friend, it's what's inside that counts! So make sure what's inside is pure. And make sure what's on the outside (your clothes, your conduct) reflects that purity.

A Word About Forgiveness

Just a word of encouragement—everyone fails. The Bible says "*all* have sinned and fall short of the glory of God" (Romans 3:23). That *all* means you, and that *all* means me. *All!* But thanks be to God, He extends His forgiveness to us when we fail. Dear heart, you can enjoy God's forgiveness for past, present, or future sin. Just follow the two steps we discussed in chapter 5:

- Confess your sin (1 John 1:9).

- Forsake your sin (Proverbs 28:13).

These two steps represent our heartfelt response to our sinful actions. But aren't we thankful that God has done His part by sending His Son to die for our sins? Because of Jesus' death on our behalf, we have His forgiveness. "He is faithful and just and will forgive us our sins and purify us from all unrighteousness" (1 John 1:9).

Heart Response

As you can tell, your purity is highly important throughout every day and every phase of your life. It's at the core of what makes you a woman after God's own heart. It's an issue of heart and mind and character.

Now, let's give much prayer (and action!) to these few practical ways to ensure our own purity as we look upward to God and to His divine, dazzling, holy purity.

✓ **A**cknowledge God's standard.

✓ **A**ssume God's standard as your standard.

✓ **A**dmit any and all sin against God's standard.

✓ **A**void compromising situations.

✓ **A**void compromising people.

✓ **A**sk for accountability.

✓ **A**cknowledge the consequences impurity reaps.

✓ **A**spire to a life of obedience—a holy life has a voice!

Things to Do Today to Develop a Heart Marked by Purity

♡ Look up the words "pure" and "purity" in an English dictionary. Write out the definitions. Then put them into your own words.

♡ Just for one day, monitor your thoughts and conversations. What did you discover? Were they pure? Do you need to make any changes? What changes?

♡ As you think about the words we've been covering in this chapter regarding purity, can you pinpoint any areas of your life that would not pass a purity test? Go through the "steps for forgiveness" and then make radical changes!

♡ Pray the prayer on the next page as often as you need to in order to help you remain pure in body, soul, and spirit.

My Prayer for Purity

Lord...

I give You all the desires of my heart—
    may You bring them into line with
    Your perfect will.

I give You my mind—
    may it be filled with thoughts that could be brought
    into Your holy presence

I give You my mouth—
    may I speak only that which honors You,
    encourages others, and reveals a pure heart.

I give You my body—
    may I keep my body pure so that it is
    a holy and honorable vessel, fit for Your use.

I give You my friendships with young men—
    may I set my heart on purity.
    May You have authority over all my passions.

I give myself afresh to You.
    Take my life and let it be
    ever, always, pure for Thee.

Would You Like to Know More?
Check It Out

✓ Read (or better yet, memorize!) Psalm 119:9-11. What question is asked, and what answer(s) is given? What is God's message to your heart? And what will you do about it?

✓ During the next month read one chapter of the book of Proverbs each day, the chapter that corresponds to the date of the month. As you read, make two lists—a list of the character traits and actions of "the wise man or woman" and a list of the character traits and actions of "the foolish man or woman." Your goal is to take note of the kind of person you are and want to be, the kind of people you want for friends, the kind of friend you want to be, and the kind of man you would want to marry.

Part Three

The Practice
of God's Priorities

15

A Heart That Belongs to God

Set your hearts on things above,
where Christ is seated at
the right hand of God.

Colossians 3:1

Congratulations! You made it! Thank you soooo much for hanging in there with me. I know we've covered a lot of ground. But my goal in writing this book was to look at the major areas of your life as a young woman and then see what God says about each one of them in His Word. Then you would have, as the cover of your book says, "a guide to friends, faith, family, and the future." Hopefully by now you have a better understanding of God's guidelines for each of these important areas of your life.

And now it's your turn. It's your turn to make these truths real in your own life. I know you want to. So please, I beg you, don't hold back. Follow the three steps—my three final words to you—that follow. They are meant to help you set your heart on things above, where Christ is seated at the right hand of God (Colossians 3:1).

Final Word #1: Kick It Up!

When I say "Kick It Up!" I'm referring to the catch-phrase used by Chef Emeril on his televised cooking program on The Food Channel. This chef has a *very* dynamic personality (and that's putting it mildly!). And when he's preparing food, he teaches his audience that there is food...and then there is *food!* He instructs those who cook that they can fix food that is okay...or they can fix food that knocks the socks off of those who eat it, food that is outstanding, above par, off the scale, in another category. How can one accomplish this? Chef Emeril says it's simple—just "kick it up a notch!" Just add the spices that kick up the flavor. Go over the edge with seasonings that make each dish memorable, the best it can be.

Well, my faithful reading friend, as we end our time together in this book about being a young woman after God's own heart, that's what I want for you (and me, too). When it comes to developing a heart that belongs to God, I want you to "kick it up a notch" and be forever kicking it up a notch. I want you to "*love* the Lord your God with *all* your heart and with *all* your soul and with *all* your strength and with *all* your mind" just like Jesus said to do in Luke 10:27. I want you to love *Him* more than you love anyone else or anything else in your life, including yourself.

I'm going to ask you to dream about your future in a minute, but do you want to know what my dream for you is? I dream (and hope and pray) that you will sell-out to Christ—now, not later. That you will step over any and all lines to follow Christ—now, not later. That you will passionately and wholeheartedly embrace His plan for your life and that you will live that plan "to the hilt"! That you will be consumed with living for God and serving the Lord—now, not later.

Oh, precious one, don't tolerate any holding patterns in your life or your spiritual growth. Don't put your heart on hold. Don't wait for something to happen, to change, to pass, or to improve. You don't have a day...or even a minute!...to lose. I just finished reading again a book written by a woman I heard speak at my church some years ago. It's a book that details the death of her lovely teenage daughter Kathi. And the title of the book? *18...No Time to Waste.* Dear one, Kathi was 18 when she and two other teenagers were killed in a car wreck.[23] So my plea to you is, don't wait on anything—sell out *now.* Kick it up a notch *now.* Do whatever you have to do to be a woman whose heart belongs to God *now.* Truly, there is no time to waste.

Final Word #2: Look Up!

A woman with a heart that belongs to God makes sure that her relationship with God is growing each day by looking to God through His Word and by praying. This is the upward look, dear heart. As you look to God for His wisdom, guidance, and strength each day by looking into His Word, and as you look to Him about the course of your life through prayer, you look up. You look full into His wonderful heart.

That's what the Word of God is, you know—it's His heart. And reading God's Word is how you can hear His heart. David put it this way in one of his psalms: "The plans of the Lord stand firm forever, the purposes of his heart through all generations" (Psalm 33:11). Another translation refers to the Word of the Lord as "the counsel of the Lord" that stands forever and as "the thoughts of his heart" extended to all generations (KJV)—even yours. As your heart and soul looks up, you are marvelously transformed and conformed into the likeness of His dear Son (1 Corinthians 4:18 and Romans 8:29).

Now here's an assignment for you, shot straight from God's heart to yours—"set your hearts on things above, where Christ is seated at the right hand of God. Set your minds on things above, not on earthly things" (Colossians 3:1-2). So exactly how do we set our hearts on things above? How do we resist the pull of earthly things? Answer: We look up. We look into God's Word. And we pray.

In years past sailors guided their ships with the aid of the stars. As they looked up, they could get their bearings and chart their path by studying the positioning of the stars. But when it was cloudy and the stars were hidden from sight, these seafarers became hopelessly lost because they had no point of reference. It's the same way for you and me. When we look up into the face of God by prayerfully reading and studying His Word, we have a point of reference to guide the ship of our life. Otherwise, we can become hopelessly lost.

I'm sure you've heard Christians give testimonies saying things like…

I wandered off the path…

I became like the prodigal son…

I fell away from the Lord…

I got sidetracked in sin…

I lost my first love…

I strayed from the truth…

I made some wrong decisions…

I went off the deep end…

I got in with the wrong crowd…

Do you ever wonder, *What happened?* How does someone wander off the path? How does a prodigal become a prodigal? How do we become sidetracked? How does one lose his or her first love, stray from the truth, begin making wrong decisions and mistakes? What leads up to going off the deep end, leaving the flock of God, choosing a lifestyle of wallowing in the mire, and eating the husks meant for pigs, like the prodigal did?

We both know what happened, don't we? Somehow, at some time, for some reason, God's Word took a secondary place to other pursuits. The lesser choices were made regarding how time was spent, until time was not taken each day to develop a passion for knowing God's plan and for following after His heart.

So look up! Prayerfully read your Bible each and every day. This one act will reveal the direction you are headed in, will point you in the direction you must go, and will help you to make the needed corrections along the way.

Beloved, at the heart of a woman seeking to live out God's plan for her life is a passion for God's Word. And when you and I fail to purposefully and willfully develop this passion, we begin to spend our precious time and days on lesser pursuits...which can lead to wandering off the path of God's purpose for our lives and out of His will. Therefore do whatever it takes to develop a passion for God's Word and the disciplines that will fuel in your heart an intense passion for the Bible.

Final Word #3: Dream On!

Motivation is key when it comes to nurturing a heart of devotion, and dreaming helps motivate us. As a wake-up call to the seriousness of daily life and to find fresh urgency about your walk with the Lord, I would like to ask you as we end our time together to dream, to *dream of being a woman after God's heart!* So to get your dreaming muscles into motion, here are a few exercises. Send up a heartfelt prayer to God and then let the answers put wings on your dreams.

♡ *Describe the woman you want to be spiritually in one year.* Do you realize that within one year you could attack a weak area in your Christian life and gain the victory? You could read through the entire Bible. You could be discipled by an older woman—or disciple a younger sister in Christ yourself (Titus 2:3-5). You could attend a Bible study for a dozen months. You could read 12 quality Christian books. And, of course, you could finish another year of school. But what *kind* of year?

♡ *Describe the woman you want to be spiritually in ten years.* Jot down your age right here right now. Just write it in the margin. Then add ten years to that figure and write that number down, too. Are you shocked? I mean, you are looking at a number that represents one year of your life multiplied ten times! Not to mention the multitude of new stages and phases that you'll pass through and enter between now and then. I admit, it's staggering!

Imagine now what those intervening ten years might hold, and you'll see that you will need God for the events of those years! You will need God to help you overcome areas of sin and grow spiritually. You will need Him in order to be His kind of daughter and sister. You will need Him to help you remain pure. You will need Him when you become a wife (if that's His will). And perhaps a mom (again, if that's His will). You will need Him should you continue being single (once again, if that's His will). You will need God to help you successfully serve others. You will need God if you enter college, Christian service, or the work force. And, dear one, you will need God should you die, if, like Kathi, that is God's plan for you. After all, yours is not only a heart but a *life* that belongs to God!

Do you believe you can be this woman? With God's grace and in His strength you can! That's His role in your life.

But there is also a place for your effort. As Scripture says, "[*You*] guard your heart, for it is the wellspring of life" (Proverbs 4:23). *You* determine some elements of the heart. *You* decide what you will or will not do, whether you will or will not grow. *You* also decide the rate at which you will grow—the hit-and-miss rate, the measles rate (a sudden rash here and there), the five-minutes-a-day rate, or the 30-minutes-a-day rate. *You* decide if you want to be a mushroom—which appears for a night and shrivels away at the first hint of wind or heat—or an oak tree, which lasts and lasts and lasts, becoming stronger and mightier with each passing year. So my question to you is, How far…and how fast…do you want to move toward becoming the woman of your dreams, a woman after God's own heart?

Heart Response

Well, my precious young traveling companion, here we are—two women with hearts after God, dreaming of "more love to Thee, O Christ, more love to Thee!" Here we stand, after looking to God's Word to find out what His heart's desire is for our hearts. Oh, what joy is ours when we submit ourselves to God and allow Him to grow in us hearts that truly belong to Him.

The future is yours, my cherished sister. My prayer for you (and me!) is that beginning today you will live each day as a woman after God's own heart. Then, precious one, every day will be beautiful in Him and for Him…until your days lived for Him are strung together to become a beautiful lifetime of living as a woman after God's own heart! And, oh, what a life that will be!

QUIET TIMES CALENDAR

Jan.	Feb.	Mar.	Apr.	May	June
1	1	1	1	1	1
2	2	2	2	2	2
3	3	3	3	3	3
4	4	4	4	4	4
5	5	5	5	5	5
6	6	6	6	6	6
7	7	7	7	7	7
8	8	8	8	8	8
9	9	9	9	9	9
10	10	10	10	10	10
11	11	11	11	11	11
12	12	12	12	12	12
13	13	13	13	13	13
14	14	14	14	14	14
15	15	15	15	15	15
16	16	16	16	16	16
17	17	17	17	17	17
18	18	18	18	18	18
19	19	19	19	19	19
20	20	20	20	20	20
21	21	21	21	21	21
22	22	22	22	22	22
23	23	23	23	23	23
24	24	24	24	24	24
25	25	25	25	25	25
26	26	26	26	26	26
27	27	27	27	27	27
28	28	28	28	28	28
29		29	29	29	29
30		30	30	30	30
31		31		31	

July	Aug.	Sept.	Oct.	Nov.	Dec.
1	1	1	1	1	1
2	2	2	2	2	2
3	3	3	3	3	3
4	4	4	4	4	4
5	5	5	5	5	5
6	6	6	6	6	6
7	7	7	7	7	7
8	8	8	8	8	8
9	9	9	9	9	9
10	10	10	10	10	10
11	11	11	11	11	11
12	12	12	12	12	12
13	13	13	13	13	13
14	14	14	14	14	14
15	15	15	15	15	15
16	16	16	16	16	16
17	17	17	17	17	17
18	18	18	18	18	18
19	19	19	19	19	19
20	20	20	20	20	20
21	21	21	21	21	21
22	22	22	22	22	22
23	23	23	23	23	23
24	24	24	24	24	24
25	25	25	25	25	25
26	26	26	26	26	26
27	27	27	27	27	27
28	28	28	28	28	28
29	29	29	29	29	29
30	30	30	30	30	30
31	31		31		31

Notes

1. Carole Mayhall, *From the Heart of a Woman* (Colorado Springs: NavPress, 1976), pp. 10-11.
2. Slightly adapted from Ray and Anne Ortlund, *The Best Half of Life* (Glendale, CA: Regal Books, 1976), pp. 24-25.
3. Ray and Anne Ortlund, *The Best Half of Life,* p. 79.
4. Jim Downing, *Meditation, The Bible Tells You How* (Colorado Springs: NavPress, 1976), pp. 15-16.
5. Robert D. Foster, *The Navigator* (Colorado Springs: NavPress, 1983), pp. 110-11.
6. Corrie ten Boom, *Don't Wrestle, Just Nestle* (Old Tappan, NJ: Fleming H. Revell Company, 1978), p. 79.
7. Oswald Chambers, *Christian Disciplines* (Grand Rapids, MI: Discovery House Publishers, 1995), p. 117.
8. Curtis Vaughan, ed., *The Old Testament Books of Poetry from 26 Translations* (Grand Rapids, MI: Zondervan Bible Publishers, 1973), pp. 478-79.
9. Curtis Vaughan, ed., *The Old Testament Books of Poetry,* p. 277.
10. Edith Schaeffer, *What Is a Family?* (Old Tappan, NJ: Fleming H. Revell Company, 1975).
11. *God's Words of Life for Teens* (Grand Rapids, MI: The Zondervan Corporation/Inspirio, 2000), p. 71.
12. *Life Application Bible* (Wheaton, IL: Tyndale House Publishers, Inc. and Youth for Christ/USA, 1988), p. 128.
13. Eleanor L. Doan, ed., *The Speaker's Sourcebook* (Grand Rapids, MI: Zondervan Publishing House, 1977), p. 176.
14. Annie Chapman, *10 Things I Want My Daughter to Know* (Eugene, OR: Harvest House Publishers, 2002), pp. 15-16.
15. *Life Application Bible*, p. 121.
16. Roy B. Zuck, *The Speaker's Quote Book* (Grand Rapids, MI: Kregel Publications, 1997), p. 174.
17. R. Kent Hughes, *Disciplines of a Godly Man* (Wheaton, IL: Crossway Books, 1991), pp. 62-63.
18. Roy B Zuck, *The Speaker's Quote Book,* p. 159.
19. Alice Gray, Steve Stephens, John Van Diest, *Lists to Live By: The Third Collection,* (Sisters, OR: Multnomah Publishers, 2001), p. 51.
20. Elisabeth Elliot, *Through Gates of Splendor* (Old Tappan, NJ: Fleming H. Revell Company, 1957).
21. Eleanor L. Doan, ed., *The Speaker's Sourcebook*, p. 114.
22. Jason Perry, *You Are Not Your Own* (Nashville: Broadman & Holman Publishers, 2002), p. 109.
23. Margaret Johnson, *18...No Time to Waste* (Grand Rapids, MI: Zondervan Publishing House, 1971).

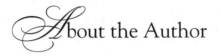

About the Author

Elizabeth George is a bestselling author and speaker whose passion is to teach the Bible in a way that changes women's lives. For information about Elizabeth's books or speaking ministry, to sign up for her mailings, or to share how God has used this book in your life, please write to Elizabeth at:

Elizabeth George
P.O. Box 2879
Belfair, WA 98528

Toll-free fax/phone: 1-800-542-4611
www.elizabethgeorge.com

~

Books by Elizabeth George

Beautiful in God's Eyes—The Treasures of the Proverbs 31 Woman
God's Wisdom for Every Woman's Life
Life Management for Busy Women
Loving God with All Your Mind
Powerful Promises™ for Every Woman
Remarkable Women of the Bible
A Wife After God's Own Heart
A Woman After God's Own Heart®
A Woman After God's Own Heart® Deluxe Edition
A Woman After God's Own Heart® Audiobook
A Woman After God's Own Heart® Prayer Journal
A Woman's High Calling
A Woman's Walk with God
A Young Woman After God's Own Heart

Growth & Study Guides

God's Wisdom for Every Woman's Life Growth & Study Guide
Life Management for Busy Women Growth & Study Guide
Powerful Promises™ for Every Woman Growth & Study Guide
Remarkable Women of the Bible Growth & Study Guide
A Wife After God's Own Heart Growth & Study Guide
A Woman After God's Own Heart® Growth & Study Guide
A Woman's High Calling Growth & Study Guide
A Woman's Walk with God Growth & Study Guide

A Woman After God's Own Heart® Bible Study Series

Walking in God's Promises—The Life of Sarah
Cultivating a Life of Character—Judges/Ruth
Becoming a Woman of Beauty & Strength—Esther
Discovering the Treasures of a Godly Woman—Proverbs 31
Nurturing a Heart of Humility—The Life of Mary
Experiencing God's Peace—Philippians
Pursuing Godliness—1 Timothy
Growing in Wisdom & Faith—James
Putting On a Gentle & Quiet Spirit—1 Peter

Children's Books

God's Wisdom for Little Boys—Character-Building Fun from Proverbs
(co-authored with Jim George)
God's Wisdom for Little Girls—Virtues & Fun from Proverbs 31